Is It My Fault, Mummy?

Also by Maggie Hartley

Is It My Fault, Mummy?

AND OTHER TRUE STORIES FROM THE NATION'S
FAVOURITE FOSTER CARER

MAGGIE HARTLEY

SEVEN DIALS

Is it My Fault, Mummy? first published in
eBook only in Great Britain in 2018
A Desperate Cry for Help first published in
eBook only in Great Britain in 2019
This omnibus edition first published in 2019 by Seven Dials,
an imprint of The Orion Publishing Group Ltd
Carmelite House, 50 Victoria Embankment,
London EC4Y 0DZ

An Hachette UK company

3 5 7 9 10 8 6 4 2

A CIP catalogue record for this book is
available from the British Library.

ISBN (Paperback): 978 1 40919580 1

Typeset by Born Group
Printed and bound in Great Britain by Clays Ltd, Elcograf S.p.A.

www.orionbooks.co.uk

Dedication

This book is dedicated to Rebecca, Albie, Ethan and all the children and teenagers who have passed through my home. It's been a privilege to have cared for you and to be able to share your stories. And to the children who live with me now. Thank you for your determination, strength and joy and for sharing your lives with me.

Contents

A Message from Maggie

I wanted to write this book to give people an honest account about what it's like to be a foster carer. To talk about some of the challenges that I face on a day-to-day basis and some of the children that I've helped.

My main concern throughout all this is to protect the children that have been in my care. For this reason all names and identifying details have been changed, including my own, and no locations have been included. But I can assure you that all my stories are based on real-life cases told from my own experiences.

Being a foster carer is a privilege and I couldn't imagine doing anything else. My house is never quiet but I wouldn't have it any other way. I hope perhaps my stories inspire other people to consider fostering, as new carers are always desperately needed.

Maggie Hartley

'Is It My Fault, Mummy?'

ONE

Where's Baby?

Big green eyes stared up at me, filled with fear. The little brown-haired girl stood in my kitchen, barefoot and in tatty My Little Pony pyjamas with her cheeks streaked with tears; she couldn't have been more than four or five. She'd got a police blanket wrapped around her shoulders but she was still shivering. That was no surprise as it was a cold, damp autumn night and her poor feet were caked in mud and practically blue with cold.

With her was Anna, one of the social workers from Social Services who was on overnight duty. Anna and I had worked together several times over the past few years so it was nice for me to see a familiar face.

'Paris, this lady is called Maggie,' Anna told her gently. 'Her job is to look after children and keep them safe. It's very late and you must be very tired so you're going to stay at her house tonight.'

The girl shook her head and started to cry.

'But what about my baby?' she sobbed, her bottom lip trembling. 'I need to get my baby.'

'Paris, the police are looking very hard for your mummy,' explained Anna. 'Once they find out where you live, we can go and get your baby for you.'

'She's obsessed by this dolly and keeps asking for it,' Anna muttered to me under her breath.

I could see this poor little mite was completely bewildered and in a state of shock and it wasn't surprising. I'd been woken up just before midnight by a call from my fostering agency asking if I could take an emergency case. The duty worker had explained a little girl had been found by a member of the public walking up the local high street, barefoot and in her pyjamas. I'd shuddered at the thought of this poor little girl wandering the streets on this chilly night. He'd called the police and all she could tell them was that her mummy had gone out and she needed to get some milk from the shop. Now, a couple of hours later, Anna had brought her here to me.

'Shall we have a chat now, Maggie, or do you want to put Paris to bed first?' she asked me.

Anna was a tall, businesslike woman who had a bit of a brusque manner but having worked with her before, I knew she meant well.

I could see Paris was exhausted but she was also terrified and I didn't just want to take her upstairs and leave her in a strange bedroom on her own.

I crouched down so I was on her level.

'Do you want to sit and watch something on telly just for a little bit while I talk to Anna?' I said.

Paris nodded meekly, her eyes glistening with tears. She followed me into the living room and I got her comfy on the sofa and covered her with one of my blankets that was softer

4

and cosier than the one she'd arrived with. Then I put on a Tom and Jerry DVD.

'Are you hungry?' I asked her gently.

'A bit.' She nodded so I brought her a slice of bread and butter and a glass of milk.

'I'm just going next door to talk to Anna now, is that alright?'

Her eyes were glazed over and she was glued to the TV. She didn't answer but she seemed OK so I went back into the kitchen.

'Poor little thing,' I sighed. 'She's shell-shocked.'

'I'm not surprised,' replied Anna. 'We don't know how long she was walking the streets for before she was found. She wouldn't say a word to the police at first. Eventually she told them her first name and that she was five but she couldn't tell them her surname or her address or show them where she lived. They drove her around the area near the shops for ages but she didn't seem to recognise anywhere,' she continued. 'No one's reported a child her age as missing, so all we can assume is that Mum's gone out, left her home alone and she's woken up and gone walkabout.'

'She seems the most upset about this baby of hers,' I sighed.

'Yes, well once we find out where she lives and find Mum or Dad, we can sort out getting her baby doll for her,' replied Anna. 'Hopefully that will bring her some comfort.

'She was found close to a big estate where there are several high rises so as soon as it gets light the police are going to start knocking on doors to see if anyone knows her or where she lives. There's also the possibility that in the meantime, Mum will come back and find her daughter missing and then she'll call the police.'

It never ceased to both amaze and horrify me that some parents seemed to think it was OK to go out leaving small children home alone to fend for themselves.

'Is there anything I can do to help in the meantime?' I asked.

'Not really,' sighed Anna. 'It's just a case of keeping Paris safe and comfortable until we manage to find out where on earth she's come from.'

I felt helpless but I knew Anna was right. All we could do was sit tight and wait for her parents to turn up or for the police to speak to someone who knew her and find out where she lived.

'I'll leave you my number and if there are any problems overnight then call me,' she told me.

'I've given it to the police as well so they've promised to keep in touch, and if Paris says anything at all that you think might help trace her parents then let me know.'

'I will do,' I said.

I saw her to the front door.

'Bye, Paris,' she called out to her. 'Sleep well and I'll see you tomorrow.'

Paris, who was still curled up on the sofa, didn't reply.

'She's shattered,' sighed Anna. 'Talk to you in the morning, Maggie, if not before.'

When Anna had gone I went back into the living room and turned off the TV. Paris didn't say a word, in fact she looked like she was in a trance.

'Let's get you to bed, sweetie,' I said gently. 'You can finish watching that in the morning.'

She looked so tiny and alone and my heart went out to her.

'Shall we go and find you a teddy so that you've got something to cuddle tonight?' I asked her.

She nodded sadly.

I took her over to the toy box. She rummaged through it and eventually pulled out a stuffed rabbit.

'Good choice,' I told her. 'Mr Rabbit is very soft and lovely to cuddle.'

I held out my hand to her and her little fist curled round mine.

'Anna told me that you're five,' I said, as I helped her up the stairs. 'So do you think if I show you where the bathroom is you're grown up enough to go in and do a wee on your own?'

'Yes and I can wash my own hands,' she said proudly.

'That's brilliant,' I told her. 'So you go to the toilet and give me a shout when you're done.'

A minute later, a little cry of 'finished' came from the bathroom. I went in and gave her hands and face a quick wipe with a flannel as she was sticky from crying.

'Do you want to brush your teeth?' I asked and she shook her head.

'I already brushed them tonight,' she replied.

It was so late and I wasn't going to push her because I could see she was exhausted.

'And you're already in your pyjamas so that saves us a job.' I smiled.

They were a little bit grubby but I thought it might help to settle her if she was wearing something familiar. Her long brown hair was matted into rats' tails but that was another job that could wait until morning. I didn't want to give her a bath as she was so tired, but her feet were filthy and I knew I couldn't send her to bed like that. So I filled the bath with a tiny bit of warm, bubbly water and got her to stand in it while I gave her feet a wash with a flannel.

'Let's go and have a look at where you're sleeping,' I told her as I gently patted her feet dry with a towel. I noticed a few little nicks on the soles of her feet where she must have caught them on a stone or gravel, but I was just thankful that she hadn't walked on any glass.

When she was dry, she followed me obediently down the landing. At the same time I was fostering a one-year-old boy called Michael who was fast asleep in the small bedroom so I took her to the bigger room where there was a single bed and bunks. I always made sure they had clean bedding on them as I'd learnt from past experience that you never knew when a child was going to turn up.

'Here you go, lovey,' I said, pulling back the duvet on the single bed.

She climbed in and lay down, clutching onto her stuffed bunny for dear life.

'I'm going to turn the big light off but I'll leave this little night light on so you're not in the dark,' I told her.

'My bedroom is just next door so if you need anything in the night then you just call me, OK? Just shout "Maggie" and I'll come straight away. Do you think you can remember that?'

Paris nodded. She still looked wide-eyed with shock and it didn't feel right just going downstairs and leaving her.

'Do you want me to sit on the end of the bed and wait for you to fall asleep?' I asked her.

'Yes please,' she mumbled.

'Night night, sleep tight,' I told her, pulling the covers up over her. 'I'll be right here.'

All was quiet until a few seconds later when Paris suddenly sat up in bed.

'Do you think they'll find my mummy soon?' she asked, tears filling her eyes once more.

'I'm sure they will,' I told her. 'There are lots of people looking for her and as soon as they find her then they'll ring me straight away and I promise I'll tell you.'

'And then I can get my baby?' she asked, her little voice filled with concern.

'Yes,' I replied. 'Then you can get your baby.

'Come on now,' I soothed. 'Lie back down and close your eyes.'

I hoped that I'd reassured her enough so she could get some sleep. Paris settled back down and I watched her chest rise and fall and her heavy eyelids flutter. Within a few minutes her breathing got deeper and she was fast asleep.

I crept out of the room and went back downstairs. It was nearly 3 a.m. now but there was no way I could get back to sleep. All I could think about was poor little Paris. What must be going through her mind? At least she was safe and sound and not still wandering the streets on a chilly autumn night. She was lucky that she hadn't been hurt or run over, and that someone decent had found her.

I glanced at the baby monitor while I flicked the kettle on. Thankfully Michael was fast asleep and hadn't been disturbed by all the toing and froing. His mum had suffered a breakdown and had had to go into a psychiatric hospital but the hope was that eventually, when she felt stronger, he would be able to go back and live with her. The other person in my house was 20-year-old Louisa who had been with me ever since her parents had been killed in a car crash seven years ago. She'd been out of the care system for years but she lived with me permanently and she was like my daughter. As a nanny, she was also a great help with my fostering placements. She was staying at boyfriend Charlie's tonight so I wouldn't see her until the following day.

I was just about to take a sip of tea when I heard shouting coming from upstairs.

'Lady! Lady!'

I bolted up there and ran into the room where Paris was sleeping. She was sitting up in bed with a worried look on her face.

'What is it, sweetie?' I asked her.

'Have you found my baby?' she asked desperately. 'You need to find him.'

'I'm sorry,' I told her. 'The police haven't found your mummy or where you live yet but when they do I'll make sure they get your dolly for you.'

'It's not a dolly,' she said crossly. 'It's my baby.'

'Yes, your baby doll,' I told her.

Paris shook her head, frustrated.

'I told you, it's not a dolly, it's a real baby.'

My heart started thumping and I couldn't help but gasp. I needed to be 100 per cent certain of what she was telling me.

'Paris, I need you to tell me all about your baby,' I said, very slowly to make sure she understood me. 'Does it make lots of noise?'

'Yes, he cries when he's hungry and he kicks his legs.'

'Has he got any teeth?'

'No, he's got no teeth, but it doesn't matter cos he just has bottles.'

10

'And has he got any hair?'

'No, it hasn't growed yet.' She smiled. 'But he has a spiky bit at the back here.'

She patted the back of her neck.

I knew by her descriptions that this wasn't a doll that she was talking about.

Oh my God, I told myself. Somewhere out there, on this cold, dark night, was a baby all alone.

'Paris, what's your baby's name?' I asked her.

'Joel, but I call him baby.' She smiled.

'And is Joel your brother?'

She nodded.

'And what was Joel doing when you left him?'

At this, her eyes filled with tears and she started to cry.

'He was in his bouncy chair but he wouldn't wake up,' she whimpered. 'I think he was poorly so that's why I went out to the shop to get him some milk to make him feel better. But I couldn't find it and it was really dark.'

'OK,' I said, trying desperately to sound calm when inside I felt a rising sense of panic. My mouth suddenly felt dry and I had to swallow to get my words out. 'You lie down and try and get back to sleep, lovey. I'm going to go and call Anna and tell her all about Joel and she can look really hard for him.'

My heart was racing and I felt physically sick as I dashed downstairs, grabbing my mobile and dialling Anna's number.

'Come on, come on,' I muttered as it rang and rang.

'Anna?' I said, when she finally picked up. 'It's Maggie. Paris is still awake and I've just been talking to her. The baby she keeps talking about isn't her doll. It's her baby brother.'

'What?' gasped Anna, sounding as horrified as I felt. 'Are you sure? She didn't tell the police or me there was anyone else in the flat with her.'

'Yes,' I said. 'I believe her. She said the baby's called Joel and she couldn't wake him up so that's why she went out. She went to the shop to get him some milk to make him feel better. From what she's said, he sounds quite little, probably under six months.'

'Oh God, OK,' said Anna. 'I'm going to put the phone down to you, Maggie, and call the police straight away. This changes everything.'

I felt sick with worry at the thought of this tiny, potentially ill baby being out there all alone. I went back upstairs and Paris was still awake. I sat on the end of her bed.

'I told Anna all about Joel and lots of people are looking really hard for him,' I said, trying to reassure her.

I paused.

'So where was your mummy when Joel was poorly?' I asked her.

'She went out,' she replied in a matter-of-fact tone, but I could see the sadness in her eyes. 'Like she always does.'

'Did she go out with Daddy?'

Paris shook her head.

'My daddy doesn't live with us any more,' she said. 'Mummy went out with Richie.'

'Who's he?' I asked.

'That's Mummy's boyfriend,' she said. 'He's Joel's daddy but not my daddy.'

I knew that while she was opening up to me, I needed to try and get as much information as possible from her that could help the police trace the baby.

'Paris, can you tell me what your mummy's name is?'

She thought for a moment and then shook her head.

'Is that because you can't remember?' I asked her gently.

She shook her head again.

'I'm not telling cos I don't want to get into trouble.'

'Why on earth would you get into trouble, sweetie?' I asked, surprised.

Her eyes filled with tears again and she stared down at the floor.

'Cos I didn't look after my baby properly and they'll be cross cos he's poorly.'

Her voice shook with emotion and the tears began to stream down her pale cheeks.

'No one will be cross with you for Joel being poorly, sweetie,' I told her, taking her hand in mine. 'If you tell us her name that means we can find out where you live really quickly then we can go round there and find Joel and check he's OK.'

'If he's still poorly, will someone give him some medicine?' she asked, her big eyes staring up at me. I felt so desperately sad for her.

'Yes, they can give him some medicine or take him to see a doctor,' I told her. 'Paris, sweetheart, it's really, really important that we find him quickly so that we can help him, so I need you to think really carefully and tell me what's your mummy's name?'

'It's just Mummy,' she said.

I knew I was probably fighting a losing battle here as many five-year-olds probably didn't know their parents' real names.

'Can you remember what Richie calls your mummy, or what her friends call her?'

13

Paris looked like she was concentrating really hard.

'Richie calls her baby,' she said, after a moment. 'But that's silly cos she's not a baby like Joel. The lady who lives next to us sometimes says Emily.'

'Emily.' I smiled, squeezing her hand gently. 'That's brilliant, Paris. You're so clever.'

I had to try another tactic to find out their surname.

'Do you go to school?'

'Yes, I'm a really big girl.' She smiled.

'I can see that,' I told her. 'But I bet you can't remember what name is written on your bag or on the front of your books, can you?'

'Yes I can,' she objected, rising to my challenge. 'On my book bag it says Paris Baker. I know cos Miss wrote it for me.'

'And does Mummy have the same last name as you?'

She nodded.

'Well done, you're such a clever girl for remembering that,' I told her. 'I'm just going to go and give Anna another quick call. You've done really well, Paris, thank you.'

I ran back downstairs and grabbed my mobile.

'Anna, it's Maggie again,' I said as soon as she answered. 'Paris's surname is Baker, mum is Emily Baker. Mum's boyfriend lives with them. I don't know his surname but his first name is Richie.'

'Maggie, that's brilliant,' she said. 'I'll get on to the police now and they should be able to trace the address pretty quickly. We'll go round there straight away.'

'Keep me posted,' I said, before the line went dead.

When I went back upstairs, I was surprised to find Paris curled up and fast asleep. I tucked the duvet up around her, knowing how exhausted she must be.

I felt sick thinking about her poor baby brother all alone in a cold house. All I could hope was that the police got to him quickly and that he was OK. I was more than happy for Anna to bring him back here so that he could be with Paris. I had a crib, baby clothes and plenty of formula, bottles and nappies.

I went back down to the living room and collapsed onto the sofa, my phone right next to me, waiting for news.

It was well over an hour later before it rang. It was Anna.

'Did the police trace the address?' I gabbled. 'Did you find the baby?'

'We found out the address and we went round,' she said. 'The baby was there.'

She paused and my stomach sank.

'Maggie, I'm so sorry,' she said sadly. 'I'm afraid it's not good news.'

TWO

A Shocking Discovery

Anna could barely get the words out as her voice quivered with emotion.

'Oh, Maggie,' she gulped. 'It was awful. The door to the flat was ajar so the police officers and I went in and we walked around and then I went into the bedroom. That's where I found him.'

She paused for a moment and then started to cry.

'He was in the bouncy chair,' she sobbed. 'At first I thought he was asleep but then I looked at his little face. I could tell straight away by the colour of him that he was dead.'

My head began to spin. I couldn't believe what I was hearing.

The baby was dead.

'I think I screamed and one of the police officers came in and checked him. He said he was definitely gone,' she continued. 'He was so cold, Maggie. The poor little lad just felt so, so cold.'

'That's awful, Anna,' I told her, struggling to hold back my own tears. 'What on earth had happened to him?'

'We don't know,' she sighed, as she regained her composure. 'There was no way to tell. There were no marks or blood on him. The police think he'd been dead for a while, a few hours at least.'

My heart sank as the reality of what she'd just said hit me like a ton of bricks. Had poor Paris been in the house with Joel when he'd died? Had she tried to wake him up and that was when she'd left the flat to go and get milk?

Anna was clearly absolutely distraught, and I could understand why.

'I'm so sorry,' I told her. 'It must have been so distressing for you finding him like that.'

'It was awful,' she sobbed. 'I've been a social worker for six years and I've never ever had to deal with a dead baby before. I've never even seen a dead body. He just looked so tiny, Maggie.'

As she cried down the phone, all I could think about was the little girl asleep upstairs who had constantly been asking about her baby brother. How on earth were we going to break this tragic news to her? It was going to shatter her little world.

'What happens now?' I asked. 'How are we going to tell Paris?'

In all my years as a foster carer I'd thankfully never been involved in a case where a baby had died.

'I've just left an urgent message for my manager explaining what's happened,' explained Anna. 'Hopefully she'll pick it up in a couple of hours when she wakes up. I'm assuming she'll want to get in touch with the police and hold an emergency case conference this morning.'

'What about Mum?' I asked.

'There's still no sign of her or the boyfriend,' Anna replied. 'The flat's now a crime scene so the police are sealing it off and forensics will probably want to take a look. There are going to be officers on duty there so if and when Mum and her partner turn up, they'll be arrested and taken for questioning.'

She described how the flat door had been ajar when they'd arrived, and a chair had been pulled up alongside it that Paris had obviously used to reach the bolt to get out.

'That poor girl,' I said. 'Do you think he died while she was in the house?' I hoped against hope that wasn't the case.

'It looks like it,' Anna replied, sighing deeply.

I felt sick. What on earth had happened within those four walls? What had Paris seen? My heart ached at the thought of this scared little girl wandering the streets, trying desperately to get some milk for her baby brother who, unbeknown to her, was already dead.

'They've taken Joel's body for a post-mortem to try and establish a cause of death,' added Anna. 'The police said the results will probably take a couple of days to come back so we won't know anything until then, but in the meantime they're treating it as suspicious.'

It was such a tragic situation but in all of this my mind was firmly focused on Paris.

'What shall I do when Paris wakes up?' I asked. 'What shall I tell her about Joel because I know she's going to ask about him.'

'Please don't tell her anything until you hear from me,' urged Anna. 'I'll ring you straight after we have had our meeting.'

'OK,' I sighed.

'I know it's going to be hard, Maggie, but we need to make sure we handle this terrible situation as best we can and that means having everyone's agreement on how best to proceed.'

'I know,' I replied. 'I completely understand.

'I hope you're OK, Anna,' I added. 'I'm here if you want to talk.'

'Thank you,' she said. 'It's all just so desperately sad.'

She was right. I hung up and looked at the clock. It was 4.30 a.m. by now. I was totally and utterly exhausted but I was too upset to sleep. I sat there in the dark living room and sobbed. I was crying tears for a baby I'd never even met, but most of all my heart was breaking for the little girl asleep upstairs and what this news was going to do to her.

Somehow I must have nodded off on the sofa as just before 7 a.m. I was woken by the sound of Michael crying. I shot upstairs to get him as quickly as I could as I didn't want him to disturb Paris.

When I walked into his room, Michael was standing in his cot waiting for me. He was doing his favourite thing of holding onto the cot bars and bouncing up and down with a huge grin on his face. He was a chubby baby with ruddy cheeks and a head full of dark curls. Seeing him, so happy, it hit me all over again what had happened in the early hours of the morning and I was overwhelmed by sadness. Here was little Michael full of energy and life and yet another poor baby had had his taken away. It was gut-wrenchingly sad.

'Good morning, my little smiler,' I said, picking him up and giving him a much-needed cuddle. I clung onto him for as long as I could, breathing in his lovely baby smell before he started wriggling around impatiently in my arms.

'Let's go get you some breakfast,' I whispered into his ear before taking him downstairs so we didn't disturb Paris.

To be honest, I was dreading her waking up because I knew the first thing that she was going to ask me was had the police found her baby brother. I didn't want to lie to her but I knew that it wasn't my place to break the horrific news. How and when that happened was a decision that needed to be made by Anna and her managers at Social Services when they had spoken to the police.

At 9.30 a.m., Anna phoned. She sounded as exhausted as I felt.

'I've just come out of the meeting,' she said. 'How's Paris?'

'She's not woken up yet,' I told her. 'I thought it was best to let her sleep as she had such a late night.'

Anna explained that they had decided that she would come round and talk to Paris about what had happened to Joel.

'She knows me from last night,' she said. 'And, Maggie, I'd like you to sit with her too when I tell her, if that's OK?'

'Of course,' I said.

'As you and I know, it's better to be honest,' she said. 'We need to tell her the truth that Joel's died. At her age she might not be able to understand it or take it in, or she might get very upset or tearful.'

'I completely agree,' I said.

I was a firm believer in being honest with children and being as straightforward and factual as possible. In my experience it only confuses kids if you tell them someone's gone to sleep, and I didn't know whether her family was religious or whether she even knew about the concept of God or Heaven.

'What did the police say?' I asked.

'So far there's still no sign of Mum or the boyfriend,' she sighed. 'They want to speak to Paris as soon as they can while everything's still fresh in her mind. As far as they're concerned, she potentially holds the key to what happened to Joel. So this morning, after we've spoken to her, they want to take her to a safe house and do a video interview with her.'

I understood why they needed to do it but I couldn't help but think it was going to be an awful lot for a five-year-old girl to cope with just after being told her baby brother had died.

'Why don't you give me a ring or text me when Paris wakes up and I'll head straight over,' said Anna, before hanging up the phone.

To be honest, I was dreading the moment when we'd have to break the news to Paris. But there was no putting off the inevitable. Just after 10 a.m. I heard shouting from upstairs.

'I'm coming, lovey,' I called up to her.

I put Michael in his playpen with his bricks in the kitchen so I knew that he was safe and wouldn't disturb us for a minute or two. Then I took a deep breath and went to get Paris. As I walked up the stairs, she was stood sheepishly at the bedroom door, blinking in the light and clutching the stuffed rabbit I'd given her the night before.

'Good morning.' I smiled gently. 'Can you remember coming to my house last night? Can you remember that Anna the social worker came with you?'

Paris nodded shyly.

'But I bet you can't remember my name.'

'Yes I can,' she said, her voice groggy with sleep. 'It's Maddy.'

'Ooh that's very close.' I smiled. 'It's Maggie.'

Suddenly the sound of Michael babbling and playing with his toys in the kitchen echoed up the stairs. Paris's face broke into a huge smile.

'Oh my baby's here!' She grinned. 'I knew the mans would find him.'

My heart sank.

'I'm so sorry, sweetie, but that's not your brother downstairs,' I told her. 'That's another baby called Michael who I'm looking after. He was fast asleep when you arrived last night so you didn't see him.'

'Oh,' she sighed, looking heartbroken, her little face etched with worry. 'Have the mans found my baby?'

My stomach sank. I didn't want to lie to her.

'Anna phoned me earlier to say she's going to come round this morning to talk to you about it so we'll know more then.'

'Oh I bet she has found my baby.' Paris smiled. 'Can he come to your house too till Mummy comes back? He can sleep in this bedroom with me. It's very big and he's only small.'

Her little face looked so excited at the thought and it took all my strength to hold back my tears.

'Let's go and get you some breakfast,' I said, trying to distract her and sounding as cheery as I could.

I took her little hand and led her down the stairs. When we went into the kitchen she ran over to see Michael in the playpen.

'Oh this one is more bigger than my baby,' she said. 'My one can't stand up like this one can and he doesn't do walking. And this one has got more hair than my baby,' she babbled on.

She gently ruffled Michael's curls and I had to turn away so she couldn't see my eyes fill up. While she played with Michael, I quickly sent Anna a text.

Paris has just woken up.

OK, she replied. *I'll be there in 15 mins.*

I poured Paris a bowl of cornflakes and she came and sat at the table.

'Am I going to school today?' she asked.

The thought of school hadn't even crossed my mind.

'No, lovey, not today. Anna will sort it all out with your teacher so don't worry.'

While she tucked into her cereal, I put Michael in his highchair and gave him some toast. Paris laughed and giggled with him and held his chubby hand.

'I bet my baby would like toast too,' she said. 'Can you make him some when he comes?'

'We'll see,' I said, unable to look her in the eye.

This was utterly horrendous. I tried to distract myself by tidying up the breakfast dishes and wiping down the surfaces because every time I thought about that poor little baby my eyes just filled up.

Five minutes later the doorbell rang and with a heavy heart I went to answer it. Anna was standing on the doorstep, still wearing the same clothes that she'd had on the previous night. She looked exhausted.

'How are you doing?' I asked her gently.

'OK.' She shrugged sadly. 'I'm dreading this.'

I gave her a sympathetic smile. As we walked into the hallway, Paris came running out of the kitchen to meet us.

'Where is he?' Paris asked her. 'Where's my baby? Have you found him?'

'I'll just go and put Michael into his playpen and you and Anna can go into the living room and have a chat,' I said.

23

When I walked back in, Paris was playing with a doll's house in the corner. Anna and I gave each other a knowing look. My heart was thumping, my mouth dry and my stomach in knots over what we were about to tell her.

'Paris, lovey, come and sit down on the sofa,' I told her, patting the cushion next to me. 'Anna and I want to talk to you.'

'But where's my baby?' she demanded crossly. 'Did you find him or not?'

'Paris, we did find your baby brother,' said Anna, slowly and carefully.

She paused and I could see that she was doing her best to compose herself. I felt the tears welling up inside me as I looked at Paris's expectant little face.

'We did find Joel,' she told her gently, leading her to sit next to me. 'But when we found him he was very, very poorly. He was so poorly that the doctors couldn't make him better. Paris, I'm afraid that Joel died.'

I kept hold of Paris's hand, waiting for a reaction, but her face remained expressionless and she didn't say anything.

'Do you understand what died means?' asked Anna.

Paris nodded.

'It's when people fall on the floor and don't get up again,' she said quietly.

I had been expecting gut-wrenching sobs or even anger, but her voice was very matter-of-fact and devoid of any emotion.

'It's when their hearts stop beating and they stop breathing and their bodies don't work any more,' I said gently.

'Is that what happened to Joel?' she asked meekly.

I nodded.

'Can you cry when you're dead?'

I shook my head.

'You can't cry or talk or eat or walk. It means that you're not alive any more so your body stops working.'

'When is he coming back?' she asked.

Anna gave me a look of utter desperation as she struggled to help Paris to understand. My heart was breaking for Paris and I honestly didn't know how to explain what had happened or help her to come to terms with it.

'I'm afraid when someone dies it means they don't ever come back, sweetie,' I told her, squeezing her hand. 'That's why we get very sad because we miss them but we can still love them and remember them in our hearts.'

'We know how much you loved your brother so it's OK to cry and feel very, very sad that you won't be able to see him again,' said Anna. 'Have you got any questions that you want to ask us?'

Paris looked like she was deep in thought and I braced myself for the difficult questions she was probably about to ask.

'Can I have some more cereal?' she asked cheerfully. 'I like Cheerios. Have you got them ones?'

Anna and I looked at each other, her deeply puzzled expression a mirror of my own. This wasn't going the way that either of us had expected it to.

THREE

Questions

In all my years of fostering, I've learnt that you can never predict how a child is going to react to a big piece of news, and it was clear that with Paris it was going to take time for it to sink in.

'Poor kid,' I sighed, when Paris had wandered off back into the kitchen. 'She doesn't really understand what it means.'

'That wasn't what I was expecting,' said Anna. 'I suppose all we can do is keep reminding her and keep talking about it and answer any of her questions.'

'It's going to hit her at some point further down the line,' I said with a heavy heart.

The difficult conversations weren't over, unfortunately, as now we had to tell her about the police interview that needed to happen that morning. Young children were not the most reliable of witnesses but at this point in time, Paris was the only witness the police had. Until we knew the results of the post-mortem, she was the one person who might be able to help them find out how Joel had died.

'The police have assured me they're going to be as gentle as possible with her,' Anna told me. 'They're going to do it at a safe house rather than at the police station and the officers won't be in uniform. You and I can go along with her too for moral support. They'll need to film it so it can be used as evidence later on if there's a court case.'

'I'll go and talk to her now,' I replied, getting up from the sofa and heading into the kitchen where Paris was playing with Michael.

'Let's get you those Cheerios then,' I said, trying to sound as upbeat as possible.

I filled her a bowl and popped them down on the table.

'When you've finished your breakfast, Anna and I are going to take you to talk to some other people,' I told her gently. 'They want to have a chat to you to try and find out where Mummy is and why Joel might have got poorly. Is that OK?'

Paris shrugged, her expression blank.

'What are the people?' she asked, her mouth full of cereal.

'They're police officers,' I told her. 'The same people who are looking for your mummy and who helped you last night and gave you a blanket.'

'But where will I go then? Will I come back here?'

'Yes, lovey, I think so,' I replied.

'Will Mummy be there too?' she asked, her eyes lighting up with excitement. 'Will I see her?'

'No, sweetie,' I said. 'Everyone is still looking very hard for your mummy but I'm afraid they haven't found her yet.'

'She'll be back soon,' she sighed. 'She always comes back in the morning.'

When Paris had finished her cereal, I took her upstairs to get dressed. Luckily I had some children's clothes in my cupboard from a previous placement. They would be a bit big for her but they would do for today until I managed to call into the supermarket. There was a pair of leggings, a jumper and a coat and I managed to find some wellies that fit her in the cupboard.

'I'll pop to the shops later and get you some things in your size,' I said. 'Do you think you can get dressed and brush your teeth now while I make Anna a cup of tea or do you want me to help you?'

'I'm a big girl, I can do it,' she replied, so proud of how independent she was.

I went back downstairs to the kitchen where Anna was keeping an eye on Michael.

'How's she doing?' she asked.

'It's so hard to tell,' I sighed. 'She hasn't said much but the poor little mite has been through so much in the past twelve hours she must still be in shock.'

'I bet she's shattered,' said Anna. 'I know I am and I'm sure you are too.'

'At least I managed to sneak in a couple of hours sleep on the sofa, unlike you,' I replied.

Just then I was interrupted by my mobile ringing. It was Becky, my supervising social worker from the fostering agency that I worked for.

'Hi, Maggie, I hear you had a tough night.'

'Yep, it's been pretty horrendous,' I laughed grimly. 'I'm assuming you know about the baby?'

'Yes,' she sighed. 'It's so tragic. Do they know what happened to him yet?'

'They're waiting for the results of the post-mortem.'

'And how's the little girl?' Becky asked.

'Anna and I are just about to take her to a safe house to be interviewed by the police,' I replied.

'No problem,' she continued. 'I just wanted to check in with you and make sure you were OK. Keep me updated.'

'I will do,' I replied.

While Anna drove Paris to the safe house, I'd arranged to drop Michael off at my friend Vicky's. Vicky was also a foster carer and she often looked after him for a few hours if I had an appointment or an important meeting. It was hard to concentrate with a one-year-old wriggling around in your arms.

'Are you OK, Maggie?' Vicky asked, her face full of concern. 'You look shattered.'

'It was a long night,' I said. 'Sorry I was a bit brief on the phone. A little girl came to stay with me in the middle of the night and unfortunately her baby brother has been found dead.'

'Oh, Maggie, that's awful,' she gasped, looking genuinely upset. 'Oh you poor thing. I hope you're OK.'

'I'm fine,' I replied. 'It's just one of those horrendous situations and we had to break the news to his sister this morning.'

'Oh the poor darling. She must be in bits.'

'She's only five,' I said. 'So I don't think she fully understands. It hasn't really hit her yet.'

Vicky gave me a big hug and said she would have Michael for as long as I needed her to. I got in the car and typed the address Anna had given me for the police safe house into my sat nav. Ten minutes later I pulled up outside what looked like an ordinary detached house on a modern estate.

I rang the doorbell and a friendly-looking young woman in trousers and a jumper answered the door. I showed her my ID.

'I'm Maggie Hartley,' I said. 'I'm the foster carer who's looking after Paris.'

'Come in,' she replied warmly. 'I'm DC Caroline Moss. My colleague Lucy is showing Paris and Anna around.'

There were two rooms downstairs and to one side was a big kitchen. It was very plain and sparse, with nothing on the worktops. I glanced in the other room, which looked like a living room. Again it was very plainly decorated with a sofa and a couple of office chairs.

Just then Anna and Paris came trooping down the stairs led by a blonde woman in her forties. Like her colleague, she was dressed casually in jeans and a T-shirt and she seemed very smiley and friendly.

'I'm DC Lucy Phelps,' she said. 'I was just showing Paris my special room upstairs.'

'It's got loads of toys in it,' Paris told me, beaming.

'Well that sounds very exciting.' I smiled.

'And have you seen what I've got in my kitchen just in case anyone feels hungry?' said Lucy, opening one of the cupboards to reveal packets of crisps and biscuits.

'Would you like something now?' she asked and Paris nodded, her eyes wide.

'Can I have a biscuit please?'

'I'll get you a nice chocolatey one,' Lucy replied, smiling encouragingly at Paris. 'And when you've had that, would you like to come back upstairs with me to my special room?'

'Can I play with the Barbies?' asked Paris.

'You can play with whatever you'd like, sweetheart,' Lucy said. 'But while you have a play I need to ask you a few questions.'

Lucy and Caroline led us all upstairs. As I followed them, we passed a huge bathroom which I noticed had a large shower cubicle and an examination table in it. This was obviously a place where victims of sensitive crimes such as rape and sexual assault could be interviewed and examined so they didn't have to go to a police station. I shuddered at the thought of what awful things people can do to one another.

Upstairs at the front of the house were another two big rooms. Paris ran into one of them. It was done out like a sitting room – there was a sofa and big plastic boxes full of toys and books. Paris happily sat on the carpet and started looking through them. I also noticed that in all four corners of the room there were cameras fixed to the walls.

'Anna and Maggie look very tired so I think they're going to have a cup of tea and a little sit-down in the other room,' Lucy told Paris.

'We'll just be next door if you need us, lovey,' I said.

But Paris was too absorbed in playing with the Barbies to even look up.

Foster carers and social workers are not allowed in the room where a taped interview is taking place with a witness, in case we're accused of prompting or manipulating them or their answers. So Caroline showed us into the other room. There were a couple of chairs and a table with a large monitor on it.

'I'll just turn this on for you so you can see what's going on,' she said, as an image of the room next door flickered onto the screen.

'It might be useful for you to hear what Paris is saying,' she continued before going back next door.

Anna and I sat in silence and watched the screen. Paris was still engrossed in all the toys and at first Lucy chatted to her about what she was playing with.

'It would be good if we could find your mummy, wouldn't it?' Lucy said after a little while. It seemed that it had been decided that she was going to take the lead with the questions. 'Do you mind if I talk to you about Mummy and where she might be?'

'Can I still play with the toys?' asked Paris.

'Of course you can,' said Lucy. 'Now, can you remember being in your flat yesterday?'

Paris nodded but her little body suddenly tensed and she picked up a Barbie and started vigorously brushing its straggly blonde hair.

'Can you remember who was with you in the flat?'

'Mummy, Richie and my baby.'

'Your baby?' asked Lucy. 'Do you mean your baby brother Joel?'

'Yes,' she said, pulling a dress off a Barbie. 'Course he was there.'

I could see Lucy was trying to jog her memory and get her thinking about the previous day. It was very hard with children Paris's age as often they had no concept of time and couldn't remember what they'd had for lunch just a few hours before.

'Did you go to school yesterday?' asked Lucy.

'No,' said Paris. 'Mummy was sleeping so she couldn't take me.'

'Does Mummy sleep a lot?' Lucy continued.

Paris nodded. I noticed that she didn't look at Lucy when she spoke and she kept her head down, concentrating hard on the dolls.

'She sleeps lots and lots cos she's had her special medicine.'

'What sort of special medicine?' asked Lucy, trying to sound offhand.

'You know, the brown one in the bag,' replied Paris matter-of-factly. 'The one with the spoon. But Mummy says not to touch it cos kids can't have it.'

Anna and I looked at each other, our expressions grim. It was heartbreaking to hear this little girl talk about the harsh reality of her home life, yet her voice remained expressionless and it was clear she was oblivious to the shocking nature of what she was saying.

'Drugs,' sighed Anna. 'It sounds like Mum was into heroin.'

'What did you do yesterday then if you didn't go to school?' Lucy continued.

'Can't remember,' said Paris flatly, picking up another Barbie.

'So you probably don't remember what you had for tea either,' she added.

'I do,' Paris replied eagerly, suddenly looking up. 'I was going to get cereal but we didn't have none so I sneaked a bit of bread.'

'Where were Mummy and Richie when you sneaked the bread?'

'Richie was watching telly but he was getting cross cos my baby was crying and he couldn't hear his football. I told Joel to shush but he didn't listen.'

'How did you know Richie was cross?' asked Lucy.

'Cos he was shouty and banging things,' she said.

'Does he often get cross?'

Paris nodded sadly.

'Does he ever get cross with you?' Lucy asked gently.

Paris nodded again.

'One time he pushed me and I fell over and got a big ouch on my leg so after that I knew I had to always be very quiet.'

'Oh dear,' sighed Lucy. 'That must have really hurt.'

Paris nodded and my heart bled for all that this little girl had endured in her short life.

'So, Paris, can you remember what happened after Richie got cross last night?'

'My baby had been naughty so Richie took him into Mummy's bedroom.'

'How did he take him?' asked Lucy. 'Like this?'

She gently picked up one of the dolls Paris was playing with and carefully put it over her shoulder.

Paris shook her head.

'No, like this.'

She roughly picked up the doll by its clothes so it was dangling in mid-air.

'But my baby didn't like that and he was crying and his head hitted the wall when they went out and then he got more noisier. But when Richie took him into Mummy's bedroom he stopped crying then.'

'Where was Mummy when this was happening?'

'Mummy was in the kitchen. She'd just woken up from a big sleep.'

'Did you see Joel after that?' asked Lucy.

'No,' sighed Paris. 'I wanted to go and say night night but Richie wouldn't let me. Mummy said I had to go to bed and stay there.'

'What happened then?' asked Lucy.

'I had a bad dream and woke up,' said Paris.

'Do you know what time it was?'

Paris shook her head.

'It was very dark. I woke up and went out but Mummy and Richie weren't there.'

'Were you frightened?' asked Lucy.

She shook her head.

'No, Mummy isn't there sometimes at night time.'

'Was Joel there?'

'Yes, he was in Mummy's room,' she said. 'He was in his bouncer. He wasn't crying no more and he was having a sleep. But I hadn't said night night and I wanted to, but he wouldn't wake up.'

'Did you try and wake him?'

Paris nodded.

'I cuddled him and told him to wake up, but he wouldn't.'

I felt tears prick my eyes. It was heartbreaking to think of this poor little girl trying desperately to wake up her dead brother. It was almost too sad to bear.

'What did you think when you couldn't wake him?' Lucy continued.

'I thinked he might be poorly cos he hadn't had his milk,' replied Paris. 'So I went to the kitchen to get him his milk but there wasn't none, that's why I went out to the shop.'

'Gosh, you were very brave to go out all on your own at night time to the shop,' said Lucy.

'I've been to get milk before at the other flat. But this time I got lost,' said Paris. 'I knew I had to find it cos my baby needed his bottle.'

She kept on playing with the dolls, brushing their hair over and over.

'When can I see my baby?' she asked suddenly, her eyes wide with alarm. 'When's he coming back? Is he with Mummy?'

'Paris, do you remember Anna and Maggie telling you this morning that your baby had died?' Lucy reminded her gently. 'I'm afraid that means Joel isn't coming back.'

'Oh yes,' Paris said. 'What's this dolly called?' she asked brightly. 'Can I keep it?'

I glanced over at Anna who looked as choked up as me.

'Bless her,' I said, fighting back tears. 'I think it's all too much for her to cope with.'

'Paris, thank you for answering all my questions,' Lucy told her. 'You've been a very brave little girl.'

'Will you find my mummy now?' she asked.

'Hopefully very soon,' Lucy reassured her. 'And when we do I'll let Anna know. We need to have a talk with your mummy too.'

'And Richie?' asked Paris.

'Yes, and Richie too,' Lucy told her, before leaving the room to come in to see us.

'She did so well,' Lucy sighed grimly. 'We need to find Richie and Mum and bring them in for questioning as soon as possible. It's a sad story, but unfortunately it's one we hear all too often.'

Anna and I got up and went out onto the landing where Paris was waiting with Caroline.

'Hello, sweetie, are you all finished?' I asked, trying to sound as cheery as I could. 'It's nearly lunchtime and you must be hungry. Shall we go home and get something to eat?'

36

Paris needed the toilet so while I took her to the bathroom, Anna and the police officers went downstairs. I heard a mobile phone ring and saw Lucy go into the front room.

'Can I have a word with you both,' she said to me and Anna as I came back down the stairs.

'Come on, Paris, let's go and get you a juice,' said Caroline, leading her into the kitchen.

'That was one of my colleagues on the phone,' Lucy told us. 'There's been a development.

'We've found Mum and Richie.'

FOUR

Little Mummy

Anna and I listened with bated breath as Lucy filled us in.

'Mum and Richie have just shown up at the flat,' she said. 'Mum was hysterical when she realised something had happened and the children had gone. She resisted arrest but the officers called for backup and they managed to calm her down.'

Lucy explained they'd both been taken to the police station for questioning.

'I'm going to head there now so I'll keep you both updated,' she added.

'Thanks,' replied Anna. 'Maggie, please don't say anything to Paris just yet until we know more.'

'I won't,' I said. 'I'll wait to hear from you.'

Despite everything that had happened, I wondered how this woman was going to take the news that her baby was dead. No matter what she'd done or how she'd behaved, I wouldn't wish that on any mother.

Before Paris and I went to pick up Michael from Vicky's, I quickly nipped into Asda and got Paris some pants, socks, pyjamas and a few basic items like jeans, jumpers and leggings. At this point in time I had no idea how long she was going to be with me.

A couple of hours later, Anna came round again.

'What's the latest?' I asked her as I made us both a much-needed cup of tea.

'Lucy just called and Emily and Richie are both still being questioned,' she said. 'Then, depending on what they say, the CPS will have to decide whether they've got enough evidence to charge them with anything.'

'Did they tell them about Joel?' I asked.

Anna nodded grimly.

'Richie didn't show any emotion apparently but Mum was hysterical. A doctor is seeing her at the moment so they have to take things very slowly. The police are trying to get the post-mortem results back as quickly as possible. Once they know how Joel died, it will help them with their questioning.

'But I think we need to tell Paris about Mum now,' continued Anna. 'We owe it to her to be honest and I want to reassure her that her mum is safe.'

'No problem, she's through here,' I said, taking Anna into the kitchen where Paris was drawing at the table.

'Paris, lovey,' I told her. 'Anna's come to have a chat to you.'

She looked up expectantly as Anna sat down next to her and my heart broke, knowing that she was hoping to see her baby brother in Anna's arms.

'I've got some news for you,' Anna told her. 'I've come to tell you that we've found your mummy and she's OK.'

'Oh,' said Paris, continuing with her drawing but disappointment showed on her face that Joel wasn't with her. 'Can I go and see her?'

'The police are looking after Mummy for a little while,' Anna explained. 'They need to speak to her like they did to you today to see if they can find out what happened to Joel. But I'll do my very best to arrange for you to see Mummy as soon as I can. Is that OK?'

Paris nodded disinterestedly, seemingly in no rush to see her mother.

'Is Richie with my mummy?' she asked. 'Are the polices looking after him too?'

'Yes, he's with the police too so they can ask him some questions,' Anna replied.

'Will he go to the house with all the toys?' she asked.

'No, he's a grown-up so the police will speak to him at a police station, and Mummy too.'

'I liked that house with the toys, specially the Barbies.' Paris smiled. 'Have you got any Barbies, Maggie?'

'I think I used to,' I said. 'I'll have a look in my loft this afternoon as I've got lots of boxes of toys up there.'

Paris carried on with her drawing.

'I'm just going to see Anna out,' I told her, picking up Michael.

We walked back out into the hallway.

'She seemed to take that OK,' said Anna.

'Poor little mite probably doesn't know whether she's coming or going,' I sighed.

After all the events of the last twenty-four hours, none of us did.

'Regardless of what happens with the investigation into Joel's death, Emily is likely to be charged with neglect as both children were left alone in the flat,' said Anna. 'So Paris is going to be staying in the care system for the moment. In the meantime I'm going to see if any family are around and see if any of them can take her. I'm trying to trace her biological father and I believe Emily's mother lives locally.

'I'll be speaking to Becky but are you OK to have Paris for the time being until we work something out?'

'Yes of course,' I said, genuinely glad to help.

I couldn't pass her onto another carer after everything she'd been through and I only had Michael at this point in time.

'What should I do about Paris's school?' I asked. 'She's been through so much in the past twenty-four hours, do you think sending her back to school would be too much right now?'

'Actually, I think it might be good to try and get a bit of normality and routine back into Paris's life,' said Anna. 'She only started in reception a couple of months ago and her attendance wasn't great. She was missing at least two or three days every week and they'd tried to contact Mum about it,' she continued. 'Her school is forty minutes away from you so I think it would make more sense for her to go to your local primary.'

'No problem,' I replied. 'I'll give them a ring this afternoon.'

The local school knew me well as I'd been sending my foster placements there for years. I had a good relationship with the head and as the children I looked after were in care, they always found a place for them in a matter of days.

We had a quiet afternoon in as I was still exhausted and I could see Paris was too. It had been less than twenty-four hours since Paris had turned up on my doorstep, yet we'd been through so much already. Louisa was due home that evening and when I heard her key in the front door, I rushed out into the hallway to talk to her. I wanted to tell her about Paris before she came through to the kitchen to meet her. As she was twenty now, I was always as honest as I was allowed to be about any child that came to live with us.

'What's wrong, Maggie?' Louisa asked as she walked through the door. I must have looked like I'd been through the wars.

'I had a bit of an eventful night while you were away,' I told her grimly, and I explained about Paris.

Louisa's mouth gaped open with shock.

'A baby's been found dead?' Louisa gasped. 'What happened?'

'Nobody's got any idea at the moment,' I told her. 'We'll know more once we get the results of the post-mortem and they finish questioning the parents.'

'That's terrible,' she sighed. 'Poor little girl.'

'I know it's upsetting, lovey, it's affected us all, but Paris seems to be doing OK. I don't think it's properly sunk in yet.'

'It's so sad.' Louisa looked genuinely upset. 'I'll come and say hello.'

I took Louisa into the kitchen.

'Paris, this is Louisa,' I told her. 'She lives here with me and Michael.'

'Hi, Paris,' said Louisa gently. 'It's really nice to meet you.'

Paris smiled shyly at her.

'I like your sparkly earrings,' she said as she saw the large gold hoops in Louisa's ears.

Louisa was a stunning young woman and her dark glossy bob was always perfectly straightened and her make-up immaculate. Little girls in particular were always drawn to her, perhaps because of her appearance as well as her kind and caring nature.

'Well, as soon as you're old enough to wear earrings, I'll get you a pair,' replied Louisa, laughing at Paris's wide-eyed smile.

The rest of the evening passed without incident and thankfully Paris seemed to settle OK. We were both so tired from the previous night's drama that I went to bed shortly after she did.

Thankfully, we both slept soundly and the following morning I had a chat to her about school.

'Because you're a big girl you need to go to school,' I told Paris.

'Will I go to my one?' she asked.

'While your mummy is talking to the police and you're staying with me, you're going to go to the school near here,' I said. 'It's a really lovely school and I think you're going to like it. We're going to go and have a look around it this afternoon.'

'Can baby Michael come too?' she asked.

'Yes, Michael can come with us,' I told her.

She already seemed very attached to Michael and I thought perhaps she was getting some comfort from being around a baby.

I'd already phoned the head teacher, Mrs Moody, and told her about what Paris had been through. It was important for them to know in case it impacted on her behaviour and they could give her extra support.

That afternoon we went up to the school and saw her new classroom and met her teacher Mrs Harris. She was a grey-haired lady in her late fifties and seemed very gentle and nurturing – exactly what Paris needed.

'Would you like to play with any of the toys?' she asked Paris. 'We've got a sand and water table outside or you can sit in the reading corner and look at some books.'

Paris shook her head shyly and clung onto my legs.

'Do you think you'll like coming here?' I asked her as I pushed the buggy back to the car.

'But am I coming back to your house?' she asked.

'Yes of course you are,' I said. 'You'll come to this school in the morning and then I'll pick you up in the afternoon.'

Luckily I'd got some burgundy jumpers left over from previous foster placements who had been at the school and that afternoon we went to the shops to pick up some white polo shirts and a couple of grey skirts.

'You're going to look so smart,' I told Paris, but she didn't look convinced.

The next morning I woke up early. I was worried about how Paris's first day was going to go and if she might refuse to go or have a tantrum. As it turned out, Mrs Harris had arranged for her to start a little bit later than all the other children and she came out to meet her and take her into the classroom.

Although she was quiet, thankfully Paris took her hand and went in willingly.

'Say bye to Maggie,' Mrs Harris told her.

'Bye, sweetie.' I waved as I stood there holding Michael. 'Have a lovely day.' She looked so small as she stared back at me with wide, frightened eyes and I wondered again if it was all a bit too much after everything she'd been through.

I needed to get straight back home as Anna had rung earlier that morning to say she was coming round. She was already waiting as I pulled up outside.

'Sorry,' I called as I hurried to get Michael out of his car seat. 'I was just dropping Paris at school.'

'It's OK; the post-mortem results are back and I thought it was best to come and see you in person,' she said, her expression as dark as the clouds that had rolled in.

'Let's go in and sit down,' I told her.

I knew, whatever the results were, they weren't going to make easy listening.

I sat down at the table with Michael on my knee as Anna described how the pathologist had found Joel had a fractured skull and a bleed on the brain.

I shook my head as I listened with a mixture of horror and anger.

'That fits in with what Paris was saying about Richie banging the baby's head against the wall,' I sighed.

'That's what the police thought too,' replied Anna.

'Joel also had old and new bruising over his body and a fractured leg which was probably a few weeks old,' she continued grimly.

'Oh! The poor little thing,' I gasped. Although over the past twenty years of working in fostering I had dealt with a lot of abuse cases, it never failed to shock me to hear what evil can be wrought upon a defenceless child.

I looked down at Michael sitting on my knee chomping on a rice cake and stroked his silky curls. How could anyone hurt a baby like that? Tears filled my eyes as I thought about the suffering and the pain that little Joel must have gone through in the last few weeks of his life.

'As a result of the post-mortem, Richie has been charged with murder and Mum has been charged with neglect and manslaughter,' Anna continued. 'They're being kept in prison on remand. Both of them are protesting their innocence. Mum's saying she didn't know Richie was hurting Joel.'

I didn't know what to think, but a part of me couldn't help but believe that you would know if your own partner was hurting your child. Surely you'd sense that there was something wrong with your baby? And if she did, how could a mother let her partner do that? What on earth would make you stay with someone like that? It was unthinkable.

Yet I also had to remember that this was a woman who by all accounts was regularly taking heroin, and heroin stopped people from thinking and feeling. It controlled everything.

'The whole thing is horrendous,' sighed Anna. 'My managers have been looking into the case and the family weren't on Social Service's radar. There were no warning signs during pregnancy and Joel had had all his health checks at birth and the first few weeks. The health visitor hadn't seen him for a couple of months but that's not unusual with a second baby and doesn't raise a red flag if there are no concerns. The family moved and it was then that things must have spiralled out of control.'

It was frightening how quickly things could go downhill.

'What should we tell Paris?' I asked.

'At this point I honestly don't know,' said Anna. 'I've never had to deal with this situation before so I'm going to have a meeting with my managers. What I am going to do as a matter of urgency is put her name down for some grief counselling so she has someone who can help her process her feelings.'

I was equally uncertain. Should you tell a five-year-old girl that her baby brother had been murdered by his dad? Would she even understand? It was still such early days and she was only just beginning to process the fact that Joel had died.

'I hope she's getting on at school OK,' I sighed, looking at the clock.

'How was she this morning?' asked Anna.

'I could see she was nervous but she went in fine,' I told her. 'I'm just worried it's too much, too soon.'

After Anna left, Paris was constantly on my mind and I was counting down the hours until I could go and pick her up.

When she saw me waiting outside the classroom with Michael in the pushchair, she came running out to see us.

'Is the baby OK?' she asked, her face etched with worry.

'Yes of course, he's absolutely fine, lovey,' I reassured her. 'How was your day? Was school OK?'

She nodded but she seemed more interested in playing with Michael.

I had a quick word with Mrs Harris before we drove home.

'How's she been?' I asked her.

'Very quiet,' she said. 'She seemed very fidgety and anxious. I asked her if she was OK and she said she was worried about Michael.'

'Michael?' I asked, puzzled.

'I assumed that was her brother who passed away,' said Mrs Harris.

'No, it's the little one over there in the pushchair,' I said. 'I'm fostering him at the moment.'

In a funny way, I wondered if this was progress. Her anxiety for Michael was perhaps a sign that she was finally processing the fact that Joel had really gone and it was sinking in that death meant that he wasn't coming back.

'Let me know if it carries on and I'll have a chat to Paris,' I told her.

I knew I needed to keep a close eye on her. A couple of days later, Mrs Harris rang at lunchtime.

'I'm sorry to bother you, Maggie, but Paris has been saying some very disturbing things.

'She's got herself very worked up and said she needs to come home as she's worried the baby's dead. Myself and the teaching assistant have been trying our best to calm her down but she's inconsolable.'

'That's OK,' I said, my heart sinking. 'I'll come up and get her.'

All the other children were having their lunch and when I walked into the empty classroom, Paris was sitting in the corner on a chair with Mrs Harris. Her eyes were red-raw and her face was all puffy and swollen.

'Oh look, Maggie's here now,' said Mrs Harris kindly.

When Paris saw Michael in the buggy, she jumped up and ran over to him. She threw herself on him and rested her head in his lap.

'Oh, you're OK, little baby,' she sighed with relief while she gently stroked his face.

'Of course he is, lovey,' I told her gently. 'He's absolutely fine. His teeth have been hurting him this morning so his cheeks are a bit red but he's eaten his lunch and he's about to go home and have his sleep.'

'But has he had his milk?' she asked, her face full of alarm once more.

'Yes, he had a bottle after his lunch.'

Paris seemed reassured but she'd got herself into such a

48

state I could see she was exhausted. She played with Michael while I had a quiet chat with Mrs Harris.

'Sorry for ringing you, but she got herself so worked up,' she told me.

'It's not a problem. She's been through so much in the past couple of days. I think it's best if I take her home. I'll have a chat to her and try and reassure her.'

When we got back I turned the TV on for Paris while I changed Michael and put him down for his sleep. Then I went downstairs and sat next to her on the sofa.

'Why did you get so upset at school today?' I asked. 'Mrs Harris said you were worried about Michael.'

Paris nodded sadly. She turned away from the TV and looked at me, her green eyes wide with fear.

'I was scared he might be deaded too like my baby.'

This poor, confused little girl. My heart went out to her.

'Paris, your brother died and that was really, really sad, but Michael isn't going to die.'

'How do you know?' Paris asked, looking like she was going to burst into tears.

'Because I've looked after lots of babies over the years and I always make sure that I give him his lunch and his dinner and his bottles, and I change his nappy and make sure he has his sleep and that he's happy and healthy.'

She didn't look convinced.

'Paris, it's my job to look after Michael just like I look after you. In the past few days I've always made sure you have a full tummy, that you have clean clothes to wear and a clean bed to sleep in every night, haven't I?'

She nodded.

'And you're alright aren't you?'

'Yes,' she said meekly.

'Well I do exactly the same for Michael, I promise.'

Clearly her grief was coming out as anxiety for Michael's welfare and all I could do was hope my words were enough to reassure her.

When I took Paris back to school the next day, I had a quick word with Mrs Harris.

'If she's ever worried or anxious like that, please do give me a call,' I told her. 'I'll make some excuse to come up to school and I'll bring the baby and then she can see for herself that he's OK.'

It broke my heart to think of her worrying about Michael all day.

I knew that it was going to take time and a lot of re-assurance. We got some funny looks from the other parents when Paris turned around one morning as she walked into the classroom and shouted, 'Maggie, don't forget to give the baby his bottle so he doesn't die!'

The grief counselling couldn't start soon enough. When we were at home, she watched me like a hawk and was constantly checking that I'd fed Michael or given him his milk.

He was playing in his playpen one afternoon when he started crying.

'Maggie, Maggie, I think the baby needs his bottle,' Paris cried anxiously.

'I think he's crying because he's tired, sweetie,' I told her. 'He's just had his tea and he's not due another bottle until before bed.'

Just at that moment the doorbell rang.

'You finish your yogurt and I'll just run and answer that,' I said.

It was someone trying to sell me something and it was a good few minutes before I managed to interrupt their sales patter and close the door on them.

When I walked back into the kitchen, I froze in horror. Paris had moved a chair and had climbed up onto the worktop and was boiling the kettle.

'Paris, get down!' I gasped. 'What on earth are you doing?'

'I'm getting the baby his milk,' she said, matter-of-factly.

'Paris, sweetie, you're five,' I told her. 'It's not your job to make Michael's bottles.'

'He needs his milk,' she pouted. 'Otherwise he might be dead.'

'Paris, look, he's fine,' I said, gesturing to Michael who was happily playing in his playpen. 'A little girl like you can't be boiling water and making bottles.'

'Yes I can,' she said defiantly. 'I made all *my* baby's bottles.'

'You fed Joel his bottles?' I asked, astonished.

She nodded.

'But didn't Mummy or Richie make them?'

'No, I did all of them,' she said proudly. 'Mummy and Richie were sleeping or gone out. I knew when he did crying that he needed his milk.'

I wasn't quite sure whether to believe her. The idea of a five-year-old making a six-month-old baby his bottle was ludicrous.

'Tell me what you did,' I asked her.

'I got the bottle and I put two big silver spoons of the white powder stuff in the bottle,' she said. 'Then I put the water from the tap in it and shook it.'

51

She did a demonstration and expertly shook it like a cock-tail shaker.

'Then I did the kettle, put the water in a big bowl and put the bottle in it until it was nice and warm.'

I was both amazed and horrified.

'Did you do anything else for Joel?' I asked.

She nodded proudly.

'I did his nappies,' she said. 'But I didn't like the stinky ones. I got him dressed and I gave him a bath.'

'You gave him a bath?' I gasped. This was all too much.

'I did when he was really tiny but then when he got too big I couldn't lift him up no more,' she said. 'Then I just wetted him with a flannel.'

This was truly horrendous. A child her age needed supervising in the bath herself, never mind giving a wriggly baby a bath. It was a wonder neither of them had been scalded or drowned. It sounded absurd but the detail Paris went into suggested she was telling me the truth.

It was becoming abundantly clear that at the age of five, she'd had to be a little mother to her baby brother because her own mother was out or high on drugs. A mummy at five.

What a huge burden of responsibility.

FIVE

Letting Go

'She did what?' gasped Anna when I rang and told her what Paris had just revealed.

'I know, it's unbelievable!' I exclaimed. 'She showed me how to make a bottle. She knew exactly how much formula to use and how to warm it up using boiling water from the kettle. Anna, she didn't just feed him, she changed him and even gave him a bath,' I continued. 'It sounds like she was the baby's main carer because Emily just wasn't capable.'

'Good grief,' Anna gasped. 'The poor girl. It's a wonder nothing happened to either of them sooner. It sounds like she was more of a mother to that baby than her own mum was.'

It was unthinkable.

I didn't want to tell Paris off as that would have been crushing for her self-esteem and besides, she had done nothing wrong. She had shouldered all that pressure and responsibility because her own mother couldn't. On several occasions I'd looked after children who had stepped up to look after their younger siblings, but I'd never before seen a child so young have that level of responsibility. I didn't want to openly criticise Emily in front of Paris, either, because no matter what had happened, she was still her mum and I didn't think it was my place to do that. A child in care is going through enough without having the added conflict of thinking their foster carer doesn't like their biological parents. It's not easy holding my tongue sometimes, especially when children have been badly neglected, but I don't like to make it into a 'them' and 'us' situation.

Most children of Paris's age like to help out with a baby but I needed to show her what was appropriate and what wasn't.

'I'm going to go change Michael's nappy,' I told her that afternoon.

'Can I do it, Maggie? Can I please do it?' she begged.

'What would be really helpful is if you could go and get me a nappy and lay it out on the change mat for me,' I told her. 'Then I can do the rest.'

She ran off straight away and got one from upstairs.

'Wow, you're such a good helper,' I praised when she came back.

'I can do it, you know, Maggie,' she said. 'I did my baby's nappies all the time.'

'I know you can,' I replied. 'But I'm the adult and it's my job to look after you and Michael and that means I do the baths and the nappies and the bottles and make your food. I'm so lucky that you're here to help me but it's important that the grown-up is in charge.'

I only hoped that in time that Paris would understand.

*

The following day I went to put a wash on in the kitchen. I was just loading up the machine when a high-pitched scream came from the living room, followed by Michael wailing.

Oh no, what's happened?

I went flying in, my heart thumping out of my chest, to find Paris curled up in the corner sobbing. Michael was still sitting on the floor with his toys where I'd left him, but now he was yelling.

'Gosh that's a lot of noise, little one,' I soothed, scooping him up into my arms.

He soon stopped crying and I was reassured that it was nothing serious. Paris, however, was in a far worse state. She was curled up in a ball, her eyes closed tight as she sobbed.

'Are you OK, sweetie?' I asked gently. 'What happened?'

'It's all my fault,' she sobbed, her little body trembling. 'I deaded my baby, now I've deaded this one.'

My heart shattered into tiny pieces. This poor child blamed herself for Joel's death.

'Paris, open your eyes,' I said calmly. 'Michael is absolutely fine. Look at him.'

She opened her eyes cautiously as if she didn't believe me. I could see the relief on her face as she saw Michael wriggling around in my arms.

'Now, tell me what happened.'

'I thought I'd deaded him,' she snivelled sadly. 'I tripped on a toy and fell on him. But it was an accident, Maggie. I wasn't being naughty, I promise. Is he going to die too?'

She started to cry again, deep sobs wracking her little body.

I put Michael down on the floor and I went and sat down next to her. I put my arm around her, and brought her close to me.

'Paris, Michael is fine,' I told her gently, stroking her hair. 'Look, he's playing with his toys now. I think you probably gave him a bit of a shock and you might have given him a very little ouch but he's OK. It was an accident, and accidents happen.'

I took her hands in mine and looked at her frightened little face.

'You didn't hurt Michael and you didn't hurt your baby,' I told her. 'I know that you loved Joel very much. You were the one who made sure he had milk and clean clothes and a clean nappy. You were a mummy and a big sister to him.'

'But I deaded him,' she sobbed, big tears rolling down her face and dampening my cardigan.

'Paris, you've got to listen to me,' I urged her, pulling her even tighter into my embrace. 'It wasn't your fault your baby died.'

'It was,' she snapped crossly, pushing herself away from me. 'Richie wouldn't let me give him his night night bottle. Then I went to bed and when I woked up he was poorly. And now he's never coming back and it's all my fault.'

She dissolved into sobs and let me hold her once more. I could see it was finally sinking in that Joel was gone but it was devastating to think that she was shouldering the blame for his death.

'Joel got poorly because he hurt his head, not because he didn't have his bottle,' I told her. 'The doctors who tried to help Joel know that, the police know that and Anna and I do too.'

'Will the polices come and get me cos I deaded my baby?' she gasped, her blue eyes wide with fear.

'No, sweetie, of course they won't,' I said. 'They're talking to Richie and Mummy because they are the grown-ups and it was their job to keep you and Joel safe, not yours.

'You have to listen to me when I say what happened to Joel wasn't your fault. It's grown-ups that look after babies, not other children. You did the best you could when Mummy had her special medicine. Do you believe me?'

She nodded reluctantly, her eyes filled with tears. But I wasn't sure the message had really got through. The poor child had been torturing herself believing Joel's death was her fault. What a huge burden to carry on such small shoulders.

I wrapped my arms around her and gently rocked her until I felt her body relax and her tears dry up. All I could do was constantly reiterate the message that she wasn't to blame and that adults were the ones who had responsibility for children.

That night as we went upstairs to do bedtime, I said to Paris, 'Why am I giving Michael a bath and not you?'

Paris shrugged, looking uncertain.

'Because I'm the big person in this house,' I reminded her. 'I'm the adult and adults look after children and do things for them.'

'I can do a bath,' said Paris.

'But it wouldn't be safe for you or for Michael,' I said. 'You're a little person and little people need big people to look after them until they're grown up and they can do it themselves.'

But Paris look puzzled.

'Why didn't my mummy look after Joel like you look after Michael?' she asked.

'Because your mummy was very tired and she had lots of other things going on and she forgot to ask other adults for help,' I replied. 'And you were being a very kind girl and doing everything you could to help her.'

That night after Paris fell quickly to sleep, the day's events having drained all her energy, I called Anna and told her what had happened.

'What a burden that poor kid has been carrying round,' sighed Anna. 'How could she believe that she killed the baby?'

'I know, it's heartbreaking, but I'll keep on reassuring her as best I can,' I said. 'The sooner she gets that grief counselling, the better. It would be good to have another person try to help her understand that it's not her fault.'

However, I knew that it could take weeks or even months to sort out grief counselling, even in an urgent case like this, as sadly the demand for it was so high. I just hoped against hope that the message would eventually sink in.

Paris had been with me for a month when we had a review meeting one morning at my house. My supervising social worker Becky was there, as well as Anna and Paris's independent reviewing officer (IRO) – a woman called Gabby who I'd worked with on cases with before. An IRO was usually a social worker, although someone not directly involved in this case, who checked that the child's needs were being met. Gabby was a very smartly dressed woman who I guessed was in her fifties. She was one of those people who you'd describe as a force of nature and she was always full of energy and ideas. It was a chance for us all to get together and talk about where things were at and how Paris was doing.

'Obviously Paris's mum Emily and her partner Richie are not able to attend as they're still in prison on remand,' Anna began. 'They will be there at least until their trial.'

She went on to explain that she had been looking into what family were around who might be able to take Paris into their home.

'I've spoken to her maternal grandma,' she said. 'Her and Emily were estranged and haven't spoken for years. To be honest, Gran's lifestyle is far from ideal and there's a history of domestic violence there with her current partner.'

'It doesn't sound like that's an option,' agreed Gabby.

However, Anna had had more success with Paris's biological dad Chris who had parental responsibility now Mum was in prison.

'We had a long chat on the phone,' said Anna. 'The poor guy was really choked up to hear what had happened to baby Joel.'

She explained how Chris had had regular contact with Paris up until three months ago.

'By all accounts things had started to slide when she met Richie around eighteen months ago,' Anna told us.

'Emily started getting funny about Chris seeing Paris and then three months ago he went round to the flat one day to find that they'd moved. He texted Emily and tried to ring but there was no response. His own partner Karen has just had a baby so he was a bit sidetracked but a few weeks ago he saw a solicitor to talk about how to go about finding Emily and get access to Paris.'

Chris lived in a town a couple of hours away and it all sounded really positive.

'I'm going to see him next week to get his thoughts,' said Anna. 'Then we can organise contact so they can start seeing each other.'

'That's great news,' I said. 'But I won't say anything to Paris until you've been to see him.'

The other matter that we needed to discuss was Joel's funeral.

'I believe the coroner has released the baby's body for burial,' said Gabby. 'It's going to be paid for by the local authority as the parents are unable to fund it themselves. Both of them have been given permission to attend.'

The question that we needed to answer was whether Paris should be allowed to go.

'I've talked to my managers at length and we've all thought long and hard about it but we don't feel it's appropriate,' said Anna. 'For a start, her mum and Richie will be there and it will be the first time that she's seen them since this happened. Emotions will be running high and we don't know how any of them will react.'

'I agree with you.' Gabby nodded. 'I personally don't think a five-year-old would have much understanding of what a funeral is.'

'What do you think, Maggie?'

I knew my feelings were irrelevant really as Social Services had pretty much decided what was going to happen and I had to abide by that.

'To be honest I don't know what I think,' I sighed. 'It's hard enough trying to help Paris understand what death means. Maybe going to a funeral would confuse her even more? But on the other hand, some people say even young children should be allowed to go because it helps bring them closure.'

'It is a tricky one,' agreed Gabby, 'but I think the overall opinion seems to be that it's best for Paris not to attend.'

In the end I felt that it was the right decision. Maybe in the future when she was older she could go and visit Joel's grave, but at this point in time it wasn't appropriate.

'As far as long-term options for Paris go, all we can do now is hope that her biological father is suitable and wants to take her on,' said Gabby.

I nodded gravely in agreement.

A few days after the review meeting, Anna came round to see me clutching a cardboard box.

'I wanted to bring these things over for Paris,' she said.

She explained that the police had finally finished with the flat and it was no longer a crime scene. As it was in Richie's name and he was in prison, the council was going to clear it within the next few weeks.

'The council gave me permission to go in,' she said. 'To be honest, it was a mess and there wasn't much of any use but I managed to grab a few things I thought Paris might like.'

One of them was a photograph. It was crumpled and the photo itself was a bit blurry but it showed a smiling Paris sitting on a swing holding her baby brother on her knee.

It was the first time that I'd seen a picture of Joel. He had the same thick brown hair as his sister and a big gummy smile.

'Oh look at him,' I sighed, feeling a lump in my throat. 'What a gorgeous boy. He's got the same lovely thick hair as Paris.'

'Yes, Mum's a brunette so they must get it from her,' said Anna.

I could see the sadness in Anna's eyes as she looked at the photo and I could tell she was thinking of the day she had found Joel's body. I knew that it was something she was going to remember for the rest of her life.

'There are a few other bits in here so I'll leave them with you to give to Paris,' she told me.

As soon as Paris came home from school, I sat her down and showed her the box.

'Anna came round today with a few things for you,' I said. 'She got them from your old flat and thought you might like them.'

I got out a furry cream blanket that had a teddy bear on it.

'Oh!' gasped Paris, breaking into a huge grin. 'That's my baby's special blanket.'

She clutched it tightly to her chest and rubbed the soft fleecy fabric against her cheek, breathing in its smell.

'Is my baby going to come and live here now?' she asked, her little face full of hope.

My heart sank at the thought of having to go through this all again but I knew I had to be patient with her.

'Paris, do you remember what we said about the doctors not being able to make Joel better? That sadly he died?'

She nodded.

'And do you remember that when someone dies, it means they're not coming back, sweetie?'

'Yes I know,' she sighed sadly.

She clearly just needed it confirming again.

'Anna also found this lovely photograph,' I said, passing it to her.

Paris studied it carefully. She looked so sad, it was as if her heart was going to break.

'My baby was very little there,' she said quietly, her voice almost a whisper. 'We were in the park. That's the first time he went on a swing.'

'If you like we could get a nice frame and you could put the photo in it?' I suggested.

'Oh, I can keep it?' said Paris, looking surprised.

'Yes of course you can,' I said. 'These are things Anna got for you from your old flat. Special things that you can keep for always that will remind you of Joel.'

Because Paris wasn't going to her brother's funeral, we had to find different ways for her to let go and say goodbye.

'When people we love very much die, it's nice to have ways to remember them,' I told her.

I explained how I'd bought her a special pink wooden box.

'You can put things in it that remind you of Joel or we can make things for him and put them in there,' I said.

'Can I draw him a picture?' she asked. 'I think he'd like that.'

'That's a great idea.' I smiled.

That afternoon she spent ages drawing with crayons and sticking stickers onto a sheet of paper.

'I've drawed my new school cos he never did see that,' she said proudly.

'That's lovely,' I replied. 'Let's put it in Joel's special box. Do you want the photograph in your special box too?'

Paris shook her head.

'I want it in my bedroom,' she said decisively.

She put it on her bedside table and that night before she went to sleep, she picked it up.

'Night night, baby Joel,' she said, giving it a kiss. Then she held the photo up as if she was showing him around the room.

'This is my new bedroom where I live now,' she said. 'This is my bed. There's two beds on top of each other over there but I don't sleep on them ones. If you was here maybe I would.'

I could see just having that blurry photo was bringing her a lot of comfort. It was something tangible that she could focus on and talk to. I said goodnight and left her bedroom door ajar. As I walked down the stairs, I could still hear her little voice chatting away to the photo of her baby brother. It was only when I walked into the living room that I finally allowed myself to break down and once the tears started falling, I thought they would never stop.

SIX

Taking the Blame

It had taken several weeks but at last the women's prison where Paris's mum Emily was being kept on remand had finally given the green light for Paris to visit her.

Neither Anna nor I knew how she was going to react to seeing her mum again. Going into a prison might upset and unsettle her but we'd all agreed it was important for Paris to know that Emily was OK and she hadn't just disappeared.

But how do you even begin to explain prison to a five-year-old?

All I could do was keep it simple. One afternoon after school, Paris was doing a jigsaw on the kitchen floor while Michael was tottering around in his baby walker.

'Remember we talked about you being able to go and see your mummy?' I told her. 'Well, Anna has organised for you to go and see her next week.'

'Is she still talking to the polices?' she asked, continuing with her puzzle.

'The police have finished talking to Mummy,' I said. 'But they think that Mummy and Richie didn't look after Joel properly and keep him safe. They want to try and find out more about how Joel died and they want them to think really hard about what happened and while they're doing that they have to stay in a very big building.'

I used the idea of her mum and Richie 'thinking about things' because at Paris's school they have a thinking chair that the children have to go and sit on to reflect on their behaviour if they misbehave or hurt someone.

'Is Mummy's building like Buckingham Palace?' said Paris.

She'd been learning about Buckingham Palace at school and was obsessed with it.

'I think Mummy's building could be as big as the palace but definitely not as fancy,' I told her. 'Mummy's not allowed to come out of her building so we're going to go and visit her there. I'm going to come with you and Anna is too. Is that OK?'

Paris nodded and carried on with her jigsaw.

'Is the baby coming?' she asked.

'No,' I replied. 'I think Michael would get a bit bored so Vicky's going to look after him.'

On the day of the visit I'd arranged for Paris to have the morning off school and Vicky had come to collect Michael. Anna had offered to drive us to the prison, which was an hour from my house on the outskirts of the city.

Paris was very quiet in the car.

'Is this Mummy's building?' she asked as we pulled up in the car park outside the imposing redbrick Victorian building. 'It's a castle!'

'Yes, it does look a little bit like that.' I smiled as I noticed the turret in the middle.

'I'm hungry,' sighed Paris.

Thankfully I'd predicted this and had some snacks and a drink in my bag.

'I've got a banana for you to eat now,' I said. 'Then after we've seen Mummy we can go for a McDonald's if you like.'

'Yay,' said Paris, looking the happiest she'd looked all day.

After she'd quickly eaten her banana she took my hand. I could feel her grip getting tighter and tighter as we walked towards the side entrance that was marked for visitors.

'Does my mummy live here?' she asked quietly.

'Yes, for now she does,' I replied gently.

'Where does she have her breakfast?'

'I don't know, sweetie, but when we see her we'll have to ask her.'

'Is Richie here?'

'No, he's not with Mummy,' I replied. 'He has to stay in a different building.'

We went through the doors into a stark, shabby reception area. There was an overpowering smell of chemical cleaner and the paint on the walls was scuffed and chipped.

Two male security guards behind a screen took our names and checked my and Anna's IDs and driving licences. There were no pleasantries and neither of them said a word to Paris who was clinging onto my legs.

Another guard appeared and led us through to a side room.

'Walk one by one through the scanner please,' he said.

'Do you want me to go first?' I asked Paris and she nodded, her little face pale and eyes as wide as saucers.

The poor little thing looked terrified and I knew how overwhelming this must feel for her.

'It's your turn now,' Anna told her gently. 'You walk through the arch to Maggie.'

'It's nothing to worry about, lovey,' I called, desperately trying to reassure her.

Anna ushered her forwards and she scurried through as if she didn't quite believe me.

When we'd all been scanned we were taken into a locker area.

'Put your bags in the lockers please,' said the guard. 'All cardigans and coats too. And she'll have to put her bag in,' he added, gesturing to the little pink rucksack Paris had on her back.

'Oh it's only got some paper and pens in just in case she gets bored,' I told him.

'Doesn't matter,' he said. 'She can't take it in.'

There was a sign on the wall that said the only thing we were allowed to bring into the visiting areas were coins for the vending machines in case we wanted a drink.

'It's this way,' barked the security guard as he led us through another set of locked doors into a long corridor. As we walked, the sound of our footsteps echoed around the tiled walls.

'You can wait in here,' he said, opening the doors into a huge hall. 'They're just bringing Emily down.'

They'd arranged for Paris to come outside normal visiting hours so it wasn't too overwhelming for her and when I saw the size of the visitor's room I was so relieved that was the case.

The hall was huge and set out with lines of tables and plastic chairs. When it was full of people it must have been bedlam.

At one end was what looked like a canteen area, although it was covered over and there was an unpleasant stale cabbagey smell. There were harsh strip lights on the ceiling and no natural light except for a couple of small windows that were so high up you couldn't see out of them.

'Look, Maggie, toys,' whispered Paris, tugging at my arm.

'Oh yes,' I said.

In one corner near to where we were sitting was a children's play area, but it looked pitiful. The toys were all dirty and broken and had definitely seen better days.

'You can go and play if you want while we wait for Mummy,' Anna told her.

Paris shook her head and moved her chair right next to mine so she was practically sitting on my lap. She was so close the smell of her shampoo wafted off her freshly washed hair.

A few minutes later a door opened on the other side of the hall and a woman shuffled in flanked by two security guards. She was wearing a red flannel shirt and grey tracksuit bottoms and she had a yellow tabard over the top presumably to show the guards which wing she was in. She was painfully thin and her tatty clothes hung off her skeletal body.

As Emily got closer, I saw her properly for the first time. Her brown hair was cut into a pixie crop and she had a stud in her nose. She must have only been in her mid-twenties but her face was sunken and grey, her skin was pale and spotty and she had dark hollows under her eyes. She looked like a typical drug addict who was going through withdrawal and I could see she hadn't taken care of herself.

'Paris!' She smiled as she approached us, showing her yellowy teeth. 'Hello, sweetie, come give Mummy a cuddle.'

She held out her skinny arms.

I could feel Paris's little body pressing closer and closer into mine.

'Come here, darling,' Emily repeated, her voice hoarse and sounding far older than her age. 'Let me see you.'

Paris hesitantly went over to her mum who pulled her into a hug.

'I've missed you, Paris,' she sighed. 'Have you missed me?'

'I miss Joel, Mummy,' she said.

Emily started to tremble and tears spilled from her eyes at the mention of her son.

'I'm sorry, Mummy,' said Paris meekly. 'Are you cross with me?'

'Why would I be cross with you, darling?' she said, pulling down the sleeves of her shirt with trembling hands.

'Cos it's my fault that Joel's dead,' sighed Paris, looking down at the floor. 'I didn't give him his night night bottle. Is it my fault, Mummy?'

Emily took her daughter's face in her trembling hands.

'Of course it's not your fault, Paris,' she whimpered. 'It's mine. I'm the one to blame, not you. I'm his mummy. I should have been looking after him.'

Emily paused.

'But I didn't.'

She put her head in her hands and her shoulders shook as her body wracked with sobs.

Paris looked unsure and edged back towards me.

It was uncomfortable to watch someone in such emotional pain. Seeing her daughter had obviously brought home to her what she had lost and how she had let her children down.

'Why don't we go over there and draw a picture for Mummy?' I said, desperately trying to distract Paris.

I didn't think it was right for her to see her mum in so much distress.

'That's a great idea,' said Anna, who was clearly thinking the same thing. 'I'm sure I saw some paper and crayons over by the toys.'

Paris seemed happy enough to follow me to the play area and I got her some scrap paper and a couple of broken crayons I found in a plastic box.

'Why don't you draw a picture for Mummy to put in her bedroom?' I suggested.

'Can I see her bedroom?' Paris asked.

'I don't think they'll let us,' I told her. 'But I'm sure she'd still love one of your pictures.'

With Paris occupied, I was close enough to Anna and Emily to still be able to hear their conversation.

'You can tell the police I didn't know about Richie, I swear,' she snivelled desperately to Anna, wiping her nose on the sleeve of her flannel shirt. 'Honest, I didn't know he was hurting the baby.'

Anna didn't say anything in response but she asked one of the security guards for a tissue and passed it to Emily.

'Ten minutes left,' one of the guards called out.

We had only been allowed a half-hour visit which, to be honest, I thought was enough.

When I could see that Emily had calmed down, I led Paris back over to her so there was time for her to say goodbye.

'Show Mummy your lovely picture,' I told her.

'I done some flowers,' Paris said shyly, handing it to her mum.

Tears filled Emily's eyes as she looked at it and she seemed too choked up to speak.

The security guards stood up and started walking over to us.

Sensing her time was up, Emily held out her arms to a hesistant Paris.

'Come give Mummy a cuddle,' she said. 'Bye, baby.'

'Bye, Mummy,' Paris said, burying her head in Emily's flannel shirt.

'Take care, Emily,' Anna told her. 'I'll be in touch.'

I gave Emily a nod of acknowledgement. By the time we'd been escorted to the door by one of the guards, she'd already been taken away. Who knew when she and Paris would see each other again.

As we walked out of the prison entrance, it was as if I could see Paris visibly relax.

'Can we go to McDonald's for lunch now,Maggie, like you said?' she asked as she happily skipped along beside me.

'If you want to,' I replied. 'Do you like burgers or do you like chicken nuggets?'

'Burgers!' she said happily.

It was only when the three of us were tucking into our lunch that I talked about her mum.

'So what was it like seeing Mummy today?' I asked her gently.

'OK.' She shrugged. 'I didn't really like her new house.'

She picked the gherkin out of her burger.

'Did I make Mummy sad?' Paris asked, her face the picture of concern.

'No, sweetie, I think Mummy was sad about Joel,' I told her. 'But that's OK. We're all sad about Joel.'

'But you drew her a beautiful picture didn't you?' Anna smiled. 'And she was so pleased to see you.'

After that we didn't talk about the visit. If Paris had brought it up then I would have done but over the next few days, she didn't mention it again.

A week after the prison visit, Anna went to see Paris's biological dad Chris and his partner Karen. After everything she'd been through, Paris desperately needed some stability and familiarity and it would be wonderful for her if she could go and live with her dad rather than be put up for adoption.

I was on tenterhooks the day of Anna's visit and I kept checking my phone, waiting for her call. It wasn't until late afternoon that she finally rang.

'Sorry,' she said. 'The traffic was terrible so it took me ages to get back.'

'Well, how did it go with Dad?' I asked, trying not to sound impatient. 'What did you think?'

'I think it all looks really positive,' she said and my heart was light with relief.

She described how Chris had a stable job as an electrician and Karen was a beautician on maternity leave with their daughter Ella.

'They seem lovely,' she said. 'They own their own home and everything was comfortable and clean. But best of all they want Paris with them,' she told me. 'They've been talking about it for a few weeks since I contacted them. Karen knows Paris and it was only when Mum got difficult and moved away that they didn't see her any more.'

'That's brilliant news,' I said, unable to keep the smile off my face.

They would need to do a few basic checks that Chris and Karen weren't known to the local Social Services or had criminal records, but on the face of it, it seemed ideal. However, before we arranged for them to meet up, we needed to tell Paris about her dad.

'If Paris seems happy then I'd like to start contact as soon as possible,' Anna told me. 'How would you feel about them having the first one at your house as Paris is obviously comfortable there?'

'I'm more than happy to do that,' I replied.

'If that goes well then I've said he can take her out for the day on Sunday so she can see Karen and meet the baby.'

'Brilliant,' I replied.

Anna came round to talk to Paris after school that day.

'Paris, do you remember your daddy?' she asked her. 'Not Richie but *your* daddy?'

She nodded excitedly.

'Yes, my daddy is tall but not like a giant and he has prickly hair on his chin,' she said. 'His girlfriend is Karen and she has a big fat tummy cos she has a baby in it like my mummy's was when Joel was in there.'

'Oh, wow, that's brilliant that you remember lots and lots, you clever girl.' Anna smiled.

'Did you like seeing your daddy?' I asked gingerly.

'Yes,' she said sadly. 'But I don't see him no more. Not for a long, long time.'

'Well, would you like to see your daddy?' asked Anna.

Paris smiled, her eyes full of hope.

'Yes!' she gasped, a wide grin spreading across her face. 'Have you speaked to him? Can he come today?'

'Hold your horses,' Anna laughed. 'I talked to him the other day and he told me how much he missed you and that he'd really like to see you. And he had some very exciting news. Since the last time you saw Daddy, Karen has had her baby. A little baby girl called Ella who's two months old.'

'Oh a baby.' She smiled. 'I likes babies. Can I see it?'

'Well, we thought it would be great for you to see Daddy first and then you can talk to him about meeting Ella. Shall I get him to come round here to Maggie's house after school this week?'

'Yes!' she said, jumping up and down. 'Can Karen come too?'

'Just Daddy to start off with,' I told her. 'He's missed you very much and he wants to see you on your own.'

Paris was like a bottle of pop for the rest of the afternoon, fizzing with excitement.

Anna arranged for Chris to come round a couple of days later for an hour after Paris got home from school. She was so full of beans when I picked her up. We were just getting out of the car at home when I noticed a man walking down the street. He was in his twenties with fair hair and a goatee beard, and was wearing a baseball hat and jeans.

Suddenly Paris screeched and ran towards him.

'Daddy, Daddy, Daddy!' she yelled, throwing herself into the man's arms.

I got Michael out of the car and walked over to them, smiling.

'Hello, you must be Maggie,' he said, holding out his hand for me to shake, the other wrapped tightly around Paris. 'It's good to meet you.'

75

'And you must be Daddy,' I laughed.

He had a nice, polite manner about him and seeing him close up, I realised he had the same bright blue eyes as Paris.

Paris skipped alongside him, chattering away, as I let us into the house.

'Daddy, this is where I live now,' she babbled. 'Baby Michael lives here too and Louisa. And did you know Joel's dead?'

Chris looked visibly shocked at Paris's frank tone and it was clear he was unsure how to respond.

'Yes, it's really sad, Paris,' he told her. 'I'm so sorry. I know how much you loved your little brother.'

Chris looked uncomfortable and quickly tried to change the subject.

'Well, it looks like a very nice house,' he said.

'Come in and I'll make us both a cup of tea,' I told him.

I left them in the front room to catch up with each other while I took Michael into the kitchen. It had only been a few minutes but already I was struck by how natural and relaxed they seemed with each other. So much had happened in the few months they'd not seen each other but they clearly had a good relationship.

When I went back in, Paris was sitting on Chris's lap and was stroking his beard while he read her a story. Most adults, especially men, find reading a story in front of other adults slightly embarrassing but Chris threw himself into it, putting on silly voices for the characters and making Paris laugh. But I didn't get the sense that he was on his best behaviour and was putting on a doting dad display to impress me. He seemed to relish being a dad to Paris again.

'I've got something for you, Paris,' he said.

Her face lit up as he pulled a little stuffed toy dog out of the pocket of his jeans.

'Oh you've brought Sparky to see me,' she said, cuddling it.

'This was my teddy I had at Daddy's house,' Paris told me, beaming.

I could see there was a genuine warmth and closeness between them.

I left them to spend some time together while I went to make Michael's tea in the kitchen. After a little while Chris came in to chat to me.

'How has she been?' he asked. 'Poor kid. I can't believe what's happened with the baby and her mum and that awful boyfriend. I was horrified when I heard.'

'She's doing OK,' I told him. 'It's been difficult for her to understand that Joel died and she'd taken on so much responsibility for the baby that she's been blaming herself for Joel's death. So we've talked a lot about how it's the adults who are in charge and I just keep reassuring her that it wasn't her fault.'

Chris looked absolutely distraught at hearing this.

'I feel so guilty,' he sighed, running his hands through his hair. 'I knew things were going downhill with her mum. It was the little things Paris had said to me. In fact Karen and I had talked about it and we were going to ask Emily if she could come and live with us. But it was too late,' he said sadly. 'They'd upped and gone and I couldn't trace them, and then Karen had the baby so I was distracted. I did try and find them, you know. I got in touch with a solicitor to help me track them down and then I heard from Social Services.'

'Listen, you've got nothing to feel guilty about,' I told him. 'You did the best you could in the circumstances.'

'I just want Paris back,' he said. 'Me and Karen want to give her a home.'

This was exactly what I was hoping for too. I just prayed that it was going to happen.

SEVEN

Moving On

Anna phoned later that afternoon.

'I've just spoken to Chris,' she said. 'It sounds like it went well today with Paris.'

'It really did,' I told her. 'She was so excited to see him, it was lovely.'

All the checks on Chris and Karen had been done and nothing of concern had been picked up.

'If Paris seems happy then I don't see why we can't aim for a quick handover,' Anna continued. 'I know Chris is taking her out on Sunday so how about he comes and collects her after school on Wednesday for good?'

'Wow, that is quick, but I think it would work,' I told her, my head slightly in a spin.

It wasn't like an adoption where everyone had to take time to get to know each other and settle in. It was only three months since Paris had seen Chris and Karen so it made sense for the process to move quickly.

On Sunday Paris was going out for the day with them, and Chris came in to collect her.

'We thought we'd go to the park and then head back home for lunch so she can see her old bedroom,' he told me, smiling at the thought.

'When we drop her off, is it OK if Karen comes in with me? She'd really like to meet you and say hi.'

'Yes of course it is,' I replied.

When they came back that evening Paris was buzzing with excitement.

She came running into the kitchen to see me and Louisa.

'Have you had a good day?' I asked, though the answer was plain to see on her face.

'I met my new sister,' Paris babbled excitedly. 'She's called Ella and she sleeps a lot and I saw my old bedroom and all my old toys and Daddy and Karen said I can go and live with them.'

'Would you like that?' I asked her and she nodded vigorously.

'Well, I think that sounds brilliant,' I added, breaking into a huge grin.

Paris went off with Louisa to show her the new baby who was asleep in her car seat in the hallway, while Chris and Karen came into the kitchen. Karen, who I guessed was in her early twenties like Chris, was very glamorous and beautifully dressed . Her long blonde hair was perfectly straight and sleek and she was immaculately made up. She certainly didn't look like someone who'd only had a baby a couple of months ago.

'It's lovely to meet you, Maggie,' she said. 'We're so grateful for everything you've done for Paris.'

'It's been a pleasure. She's a lovely little girl,' I replied, meaning every word.

'She's been through such a hard time and I only want the best for her.'

'So do we. We really want her to come and live with us,' she said, smiling at Chris who returned her grin.

'How did it go today?' I asked Chris.

'Great,' he said. 'She was really pleased to see her old bedroom and her toys. We were used to having her every other weekend so she's got quite a few things at the house.'

'And she loved Ella.' Karen smiled.

I was relieved. I knew that nobody would ever replace Joel, but I hoped that having a new baby to love might help ease the grief and guilt she still felt and also show her that babies should be cared for by their parents. I was glad it was a girl so things were slightly different to her experience with Joel.

Chris had already told Paris that she would be moving in with them for good on Wednesday, so over the next few days she helped me to pack a few of her things. She'd only been with us for two months so she didn't have huge amounts of stuff.

'Louisa, Michael and I are really going to miss you,' I told Paris. 'But we know you're going to be so happy with your daddy.'

'And Karen and baby Ella,' she corrected me.

'Of course, silly me.' I grinned. 'How could I forget them?'

The night before Paris was due to move permanently, we had a little leaving party with Louisa and Michael. I made a chocolate cake and Louisa blew up a few balloons. I noticed that Paris was very quiet all evening.

Change is often scary for children, even when it's positive, so I thought I'd have a chat with her at bedtime to try and reassure her.

'Are you OK, sweetie?' I asked as I sat on the end of her bed and tucked her in. 'Are you looking forward to moving in with Daddy tomorrow? You must be so excited.'

She shook her head sadly.

'I can't go and live at Daddy's house, Maggie,' she replied, tears filling her green eyes.

'But why ever not?' I asked, my heart sinking. 'You seemed so happy about going to live with him before.'

'Cos what if I dead baby Ella like I deaded Joel?' she said, a single tear running down her cheek. 'Daddy would be so sad and the polices would put me in a building like Mummy.'

I took her hands in mine.

'Paris, what have I been telling you all along?' I said gently. 'It's not your fault Joel died. You did everything you could for him. You cared for him when your mummy couldn't. Do you believe me?'

She nodded her head although I wasn't sure. It was something that needed to be explored further through therapy and definitely something Chris had to help her with too. I was also glad that Anna would still have regular contact with the family when Paris went to live with them.

'Will I have to see Mummy again when I go to live with Daddy?' she asked.

'That's up to you and Daddy,' I said. 'Would you like to visit her again?'

'No,' she said firmly. 'I don't like that building. The toys was dirty and the crayons were broken.'

'Well, when you go and live with Daddy you tell him what you think and if you don't want to see Mummy, you won't have to. Does that sound OK?'

She nodded.

'Now you try and get some sleep.' I smiled, brushing her thick glossy hair off her face. 'It's going to be an exciting day tomorrow.'

She gave me a weak smile.

As I went downstairs I felt like I always did when a child was about to leave, that feeling I could only describe as 'happy-sad'. Happy that a child was moving on to a permanent, loving home but sad that I was losing them. Paris had been through so much and even though she had only been with me a short time, I cared about her deeply and wanted the best for her.

Louisa could read me like a book and as I sat down on the sofa she handed me a tub of Celebrations.

'Have some chocolate and I'm going to make you a cup of tea and put on a chick flick to take your mind off tomorrow,' she told me.

'Thank you, lovey,' I replied, so glad Louisa was with me.

To be honest, the reality of saying goodbye was a lot easier than the thought of it. That afternoon, after I'd picked Paris up from school, was frantic as I quickly made sure all her stuff was ready. She gave Michael and Louisa a goodbye cuddle as I dashed around, making sure she'd got everything.

Most of her things had fitted into a large suitcase except her memory box and the picture of Joel that Paris insisted on carrying with her.

'It's to make sure I don't forget it and I want to show Joel my new house,' she told me.

She talked to the photograph all the time and it was clear that it gave her a lot of comfort.

When Chris arrived he loaded up the car while I gave Paris a hug. Despite her reservations the night before, I could see she couldn't wait to go. And I was glad.

'Daddy says we're going to have fish and chippys for tea,' she said, a huge smile on her face.

'Aren't you lucky.' I grinned back. 'We're going to miss you but I know you're going to be so happy with your daddy and Karen and baby Ella.'

I took a deep breath and swallowed the lump in my throat as Chris helped her to strap herself into her car seat.

'Take care,' I told him. 'Keep in touch if you want to and if there's anything I can do to help then just let me know.'

'Thank you,' he said. 'And thank you for everything you've done for Paris.'

But as they drove away, my heart felt heavy about the hard times that were likely to come. As Paris got older and gained more of an understanding of what had happened to her, my experience told me that her grief and anger would rise to the surface and surprise her. I hoped that I had helped her in some small way through the darkest months of her life. Above all, I hoped that I'd made her realise that what had happened to her brother wasn't her fault. That she wasn't to blame.

But in the meantime Paris was safe and cared for and free to be a child again, and she had a dad and stepmum who clearly loved her. And love is all you can ever ask for.

Epilogue

Seven months had passed when I was flicking through the local paper and a story caught my eye.

'Life for father who killed baby.'

It was just a small piece but the names had jumped out at me.

'After a two-week trial, Richie Tyler was found guilty of killing his six-month-old son Joel and was jailed for life . . . The baby had several old injuries as well as a fractured skull and bleed on the brain that led to his death . . . His partner Emily Baker was found guilty of manslaughter and child cruelty and jailed for six years. Baker, a heroin addict, denied knowing that Tyler was abusing their son but the jury failed to believe her.'

I was glad someone had been held to account for baby Joel's death but I still felt so sad for Paris and what she'd been put through. I never heard from Chris again and to be honest I didn't expect to. Paris had only been with me for two months and he wanted a fresh start for his new family. He didn't want to be reminded of the tragic past of his daughter, a past for which he also felt guilt.

I've been kept busy with the countless other children who passed through my door but I still find myself thinking of Paris. She will be a teenager now, and wherever she is, I hope she's found the happiness that she deserves.

A Desperate Cry for Help

ONE

Rude Awakening

There's nothing like a phone call in the early hours of the morning to wake you up instantly.

I sat bolt upright in bed and lurched for my mobile before it could disturb anyone else in the house.

'Hello?' I mumbled groggily.

'Maggie, I'm so sorry to bother you so early,' said a voice. 'It's Helen here, one of the out-of-hours social workers.'

It took me a few seconds to get my brain in gear and actually process who it was.

'Oh hi,' I croaked. 'Sorry, I was in a deep sleep there.'

'Social Services have been in touch,' she explained. 'They've got a bit of an emergency situation that I was hoping you might be able to help with.'

'Yes, of course,' I replied, heaving myself out of bed and pulling on my dressing gown.

Although it still felt like the middle of the night, I realised it was actually just after half past six and starting to get light outside. I walked over to the window and drew back the curtains, blinking as the first rays of the early morning October sun filled my bedroom.

'What's happened?' I asked.

'Unfortunately there was a fire last night at Mildred House – one of the local children's homes,' Helen told me.

'Oh no,' I gasped. 'How awful. Were any of the kids hurt?'

'Thankfully not,' she sighed. 'The fire alarms went off straight away and the staff were able to get everyone out safely. The fire brigade managed to get it under control pretty quickly although unfortunately there's still been quite a lot of damage to one part of the building – the kitchen and one of the bedrooms have been totally destroyed.

'There were four girls who shared that room so now Social Services is looking for emergency accommodation for them,' Helen continued. 'They've managed to place three so far with foster carers and I was wondering whether you would be able to take the fourth? I can see from the system that you've just got one respite placement with you at the moment.'

'Yes, that's right. I've got Isla for a few more weeks but I've got another bedroom that I use for fostering so I've got the room for another child.'

Isla was eight and was staying with me while her mother Agnes recovered from a hip operation. She was a single parent and all her family were in Poland so she had no one to help out and get Isla to and from school while she was off her feet. Isla was a sweet little thing and she'd been a joy to look after.

'I'm afraid I don't know much about the girl,' Helen told me. 'All I know is that she's twelve and she's currently being treated at the hospital for smoke inhalation.'

'Poor little mite,' I sighed. 'I bet she was terrified. I'd be happy to have her.'

'Thank you, Maggie,' said Helen, sounding relieved. 'I'll ring the duty social worker, Jan, now and she'll bring her straight to you from the hospital.'

'OK, great,' I said. 'I'll be here.'

As soon as I hung up, I leapt into action. I wanted to be showered and dressed before Jan arrived with my new placement. Just then there was a gentle tapping on the bedroom door.

'Maggie?' called a hushed voice.

'Come in, flower,' I called.

It was Louisa. She was twenty-two and had been with me since she was thirteen when her parents had died in a car crash. She'd been out of the care system for years but she'd lived with me ever since, and to all intents and purposes, she was my daughter.

'Sorry, love, did I wake you?' I asked. 'I was trying to keep my voice down.'

'I heard your phone ringing and I was just checking everything was OK,' she told me. 'I've got to get up for work anyway.'

Louisa was a nanny for a local family.

'Everything's fine,' I told her. 'It was just my agency asking if I could take on an emergency placement.'

I explained about the fire at Mildred House and the twelve-year-old girl who was on her way to our house.

'Oh, that's awful,' sighed Louisa. 'That must have been really scary.'

'She could be here any minute so I'm keen to get organised,' I told her.

'I can drop Isla off at school for you if that would help?' she suggested.

'You're an angel.' I smiled. 'I'd completely forgotten about the school run. If you're sure you don't mind, that would be a great help. I wouldn't want to have to drag the poor girl straight out of the door immediately after she arrives. I think she'll probably want a quiet morning after everything that's happened.'

Although I tried not to rely on Louisa too much, it was at times like this that she was an absolute godsend to a single carer like me. For the past eighteen months she'd been engaged to her boyfriend Charlie and although I was delighted for her, there was a part of me that was dreading the day when they'd saved enough money to get their own place and she would move out.

By seven o'clock I was washed, dressed and downstairs having a cup of tea with Louisa. Isla wasn't awake yet.

'It must be so frightening to be in a fire,' said Louisa. 'That's my worst nightmare.'

'I'm just glad no one was seriously hurt.' I nodded.

'Do they know how it started?'

I shook my head.

'Helen didn't have any other info. I don't even know the poor girl's name. I suppose we'll find out when the social worker gets here.'

But there was still no sign of them by the time Isla trotted downstairs at half past seven. She was a sweet little thing with a wild mess of light brown curls that always looked tangled no matter how many times I brushed them.

'I've got a treat for you,' I told her as I poured her a bowl of cornflakes. 'Louisa's going to take you to school this morning.'

'Yay.' She beamed excitedly, her freckled nose wrinkling with delight.

'That will be nice, won't it?' Louisa smiled.

We both loved having Isla around as she was such a sweet, good-natured girl. She was very self-sufficient and would happily entertain herself by drawing a picture or reading a book – very different to most of the troubled children who came into my care.

Just after I'd waved them off down the street at half past eight, I saw a car pull up outside. I lingered on the doorstep, the familiar flutter of nerves and excitement in my stomach that I always got when I was about to meet a new placement.

'Hi, is it Jan?' I asked expectantly as a grey-haired woman in her late fifties got out of the driver's seat.

'It is indeed.' She smiled. 'Nice to meet you, Maggie.'

I watched while she opened up the passenger door.

'Come on then,' she said gently. 'This is where you'll be staying.'

A girl clambered out of the back seat. She was shivering in a pair of pyjamas that were black with ash and she had a hospital blanket wrapped around her shoulders. She was wearing a pair of trainers that were miles too big for her so she had to shuffle along the front path. She was tall and heavyset with long dark, straggly hair and she towered over Jan.

I smiled kindly at her and she stared back at me with scared brown eyes ringed with dark circles. Even her face was smudged with ash and as she got closer to me, I could smell the overpowering stench of smoke. Poor kid, I thought to myself. She looked completely bewildered and traumatised.

'Maggie, this is Meg,' Jan told me.

'Hi, Meg.' I smiled. 'Come on, let's get you inside. It sounds like you've had quite a night.'

They followed me into the hallway.

'Are you hungry?' I asked her. 'Would you like some breakfast?'

Meg nodded.

'I didn't have nothing at the hospital,' she said.

'Well, why don't you watch a bit of telly in here,' I said, ushering her into the living room. 'Then Jan and I can go into the kitchen and get you a drink and make you some toast. Does that sound OK?'

Meg nodded.

I got her settled on the sofa and handed her the remote.

'I'll give you a shout when it's ready,' I told her and she gave me a weak smile.

Jan and I wandered through to the kitchen.

'I'm sure you could do with a cuppa too,' I said, as I filled up the kettle.

'That would be wonderful.' She smiled gratefully. 'It's been a busy morning.'

As I put some bread in the toaster, she explained what had happened.

'The fire broke out around 3.30 a.m.,' she explained. 'The member of staff on overnight duty was over the other side of the building at the time but the alarms went off and she managed to get the four girls out safely.

'There are another two bedrooms at Mildred House but that side of the building wasn't affected thankfully. The kitchen was pretty much destroyed in the blaze and the bedroom was badly smoke-damaged so unfortunately Meg hasn't got anything with her,' Jan continued. 'I've had to lend her my old trainers that were in the boot of my car.'

'Don't worry, I've probably got a few things in my cupboard that will fit her and I'll take her down to Asda today and get her a few bits. Do they know how the fire started?'

Jan shook her head.

'It's too early to know. They're pretty sure it started in the kitchen so it's more than likely something electrical but the fire service is investigating.'

Meg's toast suddenly popped up.

'Before I take this in to her, is there anything that you can tell me about Meg?' I asked.

Jan shrugged. 'I only had chance for a very quick chat to the workers at Mildred House but she's been in care about four months.'

Jan explained that Meg had two other siblings. Meg was the eldest and her mum had struggled to cope with her behaviour.

'She's been going off the rails, not going to school, staying out with her friends, running off, drinking. Mum just couldn't cope. When I get back to the office I'll arrange for her social worker to give you a call as she'll have more details.'

'OK, thanks,' I said.

There was so much I needed to know but in the meantime I wanted to make sure Meg was comfortable.

'She's been very quiet and understandably I think she's traumatised by what happened,' Jan told me. 'The hospital gave her some oxygen and thankfully she seems to be breathing OK now.

'They said she needs to get plenty of rest and her throat will probably be quite sore for a few days.'

'It must have been terrifying for her,' I sighed. 'I'll keep a close eye on her and make sure she has a quiet day.'

I took in a plate of toast and butter and a beaker of orange juice for her.

'Here you go, lovey,' I said, passing her the plate. 'See if you can manage the toast with your sore throat. How are you feeling?'

She scowled. 'I stink of fire and it's making me choke,' she coughed. 'It's all in my clothes and my hair.'

'Well after you've had your toast I'll run you a nice bath and then I'll sort you out some clean clothes,' I soothed.

I could see she was shaken up.

'Meg, I'm so sorry but I've got to go now, but I'll leave you in Maggie's capable hands,' Jan told her, popping her head around the door. 'Don't worry, Maggie's going to speak to your social worker and they'll sort everything out.'

'How long have I got to stay here?' she asked.

'I honestly don't know at this point, I'm afraid,' Jan replied. 'Your bedroom was badly damaged in the fire so I'm afraid you can't go back to Mildred House at the moment.'

'But if I can't go back there, then can I go back to my mum's?' Meg asked, a hopeful look on her face.

Jan gave her a sympathetic smile but didn't say anything.

'I'm afraid it's not as simple as that, sweetie,' I told her gently.

She looked up at me, her pale face streaked with ash. Given the severity of the fire, it was likely that she'd lost everything she owned, and now here she was, all alone with only a stranger to comfort her. My heart went out to this poor girl.

TWO

Simmering Rage

When Jan had gone, I ran a bath for Meg and dug out some clothes for her. As she was big for her age, I didn't think the eleven to twelve-year-old clothes that I'd got in the cupboard would fit her. Even the ones for thirteen-year-olds looked like they'd be a little snug. In the end I went into Louisa's room and got some tracksuit bottoms and a sweatshirt that were in a pile of things she'd sorted out to take to the charity shop. They were a women's size ten but they looked like they'd fit.

When the bath was ready, I went back into the living room to get Meg.

'Come with me and I'll show you where you'll be sleeping,' I told her and she followed me wearily upstairs.

When Isla had arrived I'd put her in the bigger room because it was closer to my bedroom, which meant that Meg would be in the smaller single room.

'It's not massive but I think it's really cosy.' I smiled.

She glanced around. 'S'alright I suppose.' She shrugged.

I showed her around the rest of the upstairs.

'Who sleeps in here then?' she asked when I took her into the bigger bedroom.

'This is Isla's room,' I told her. 'She's eight and she's staying with me at the moment because her mum's not very well. She's at school but you can meet her tonight.'

I also explained about Louisa. 'She's at work now but she'll be home later too so I'll introduce you then,' I added.

'Whatever,' she sighed wearily, rolling her eyes. 'I don't care.'

I didn't say anything or pull her up on being rude as I knew she'd been up half the night and I could see how exhausted she was.

'Your bath's ready now, so go and have a good soak,' I said gently. 'That should get rid of the smell of smoke and make you feel a lot better.'

I handed her a towel and the clothes and she gave me a grunt of acknowledgement.

'When you're out of the bath, would you like to give your mum a ring and let her know that you're OK?' I asked. I spoke without thinking, and as soon as the words were out of my mouth, I regretted them.

Meg's face immediately filled with rage.

'No way!' she spat. 'I don't wanna ring that bitch. She put me in care. I hate her! I don't wanna speak to her.'

I was shocked by the venom in her voice.

'It's OK, lovey. You don't have to call her if you don't want to,' I soothed, trying to calm her down. 'Sorry, I didn't mean to upset you.'

I was so cross with myself for mentioning her mum and I knew then I shouldn't have said anything until I'd spoken to her social worker and got more information about her background.

While Meg was in the bath, I went into her bedroom and made sure everything was ready for her. I always had clean bedding on the beds as often children arrived with very little notice, but I put a little teddy on her pillow which is something I always did when someone new came. I was just putting some spare pyjamas in the chest of drawers for her when my mobile rang.

'Hi, Maggie, it's Angela here, Meg's social worker,' said a woman's voice.

She sounded breathless and frantic.

'I've just come into the office and heard about the fire at Mildred House. How is she?'

'She's doing OK,' I told her. 'I think she's understandably very shocked but she's had a lucky escape. She inhaled quite a lot of smoke so I'm keeping a close eye on her.'

'I'm just glad she's alright,' she sighed. 'It must have been so scary. Can I speak to her?'

'I'm afraid she's in the bath at the moment. But I can get her to call you when she's out if you'd like? Actually, have you got five minutes now to tell me a little bit more about her?'

I was eager to know more about this angry young girl so that I could better understand and help her.

'Yes, of course,' she replied.

Angela explained that Meg's mum Zoe suffered from depression.

'For the past year she's really struggled to deal with Meg's behaviour,' she told me. 'It's typical teenage stuff – truanting from school, falling in with a bad crowd, drinking and smoking – but Meg was only eleven when she started going off the rails. She also started being really mentally and physically abusive to her mum. It got to the point where Zoe just couldn't manage her behaviour any more so she asked if Social Services could take Meg into care for a bit as she felt she was close to breaking point.

'She's got two younger daughters, Sophie and Laura, who were also suffering as a result of Meg's actions. Zoe was just getting more and more depressed.'

'Poor woman,' I sighed.

I was always full of admiration for parents who acknowledged that they couldn't cope and asked for Social Services' help. I knew it was something that most people didn't do lightly and it must have been so heart-wrenching to voluntarily put your child into the care system. Things had to be desperate for you to even contemplate doing that.

'Have they been having contact?' I asked.

'They did at first, but unfortunately things have broken down over the last few weeks,' sighed Angela. 'Meg is very resentful towards her mum and her sisters and every time there was a contact session, arguments would start. Meg would storm off, Mum would get upset.'

She explained how a couple of times Meg had managed to get out of the contact centre and they'd had to ring the police. Officers had eventually picked her up in the town centre and brought her back to the children's home.

'It's such a tricky situation, There's no question of neglect or abuse – the other two girls are well cared for and happy – it's just Zoe and Meg clashing, and now understandably there's a lot of additional anger on Meg's side about Mum putting her into care.'

'Yes, I asked Meg earlier if she wanted to call her mum and to say it didn't go down very well is an understatement,' I told her.

'Don't worry, Zoe knows about the fire,' Angela replied. 'I called her before I rang you and reassured her that Meg was OK.'

She explained that Meg and her family were on the waiting list for counselling. 'What we're hoping is that with some family therapy we can work with Meg and her mum and eventually she'll be in a position to go back home. But at this point in time it's just not going to work,' she sighed.

The lack of mental health support for young people was and still is a massive bugbear of mine. There's simply not enough provision for any child but in particular children in the care system, who often need it the most.

While I was talking to Angela I also needed to find out what to do about Meg and school.

'She was expelled from her old school and since she's been in care she's been taught at Mildred House,' Angela explained. 'They have a couple of teachers who come in to the home every day.'

'What will happen now?' I asked.

'Apparently that part of the building wasn't affected by the fire so she'll still be able to go back for lessons. My colleague Jan explained that you're fostering another child so we'll arrange for a taxi to take Meg to and from Mildred House every day.'

'Yes, that's right,' I said. 'Thank you, that will really help as I'll be doing the school run with Isla.'

Angela said that she would be round at some point in the next few days to check on Meg and we said our goodbyes.

'Your social worker called to see how you were,' I told Meg when she was out of the bath.

'Don't know why,' she sneered. 'She doesn't care about me.'

'Of course she does,' I told her. 'She was really worried about you when she heard about the fire.'

'As if,' she scoffed. 'No one cares if I live or die.'

'You know that's not true, Meg,' I replied. Despite her tough exterior, I couldn't help feeling sorry for this young girl who had been through so much in the past few hours.

She suddenly broke off into a coughing fit and in her new pyjamas, she looked much younger than her twelve years.

'Come on, sweetie, I can see you're exhausted and we've really got to watch those lungs of yours after you've breathed in all that smoke,' I told her gently. 'Come and have a lie-down in the living room.'

Meg didn't argue. She lay on the sofa and watched TV while I did some jobs in the kitchen. When I checked on her ten minutes later, she was fast asleep. As I quietly turned off the TV and gently put a blanket over her, I could still smell smoke on her skin. I really felt for her. I kept thinking about how terrifying it must have been being woken up in the night and having to find her way out of a burning building through choking smoke.

As Meg was big for her age, I could see how people might treat her like a teenager, but in my eyes, at twelve, she was still just a little girl. And a very lost and hurt little girl at that.

Meg must have been exhausted because she slept for the next three hours. When she finally woke up I made her a sandwich.

'My throat hurts,' she croaked.

'You must try and eat something, lovey,' I told her, pushing the sandwich towards her gently.

Reluctantly she took a few bites and settled back in front of the television listlessly.

Soon it was time to collect Isla from school.

'Do I have to go?' sighed Meg.

'I'm sorry, flower, but you do I'm afraid,' I told her. 'I can't leave you here on your own, not after you've been in hospital. I usually walk there but I'll drive us today so you can have a rest in the car.'

That seemed to appease her.

Isla came skipping out of school, a big smile on her face as usual. But she stopped dead in her tracks when she saw Meg standing next to me, scowling.

'Who are you?' Isla asked her warily, her eyes wide.

'Isla, this is Meg,' I told her. 'She's going to be staying with us for a little while.' I didn't go into details about the fire.

'Oh.' She smiled, obviously curious. 'Hi, Meg, I'm Isla. My mummy's got a poorly hip so I'm having a sleepover at Maggie's until she's better. Where's your mummy?'

'None of your business,' snapped Meg. 'I don't wanna talk about her.'

Isla looked a bit taken aback.

'Don't worry, sometimes people get sad when they talk about their mummies,' I reassured Isla as Meg stomped off ahead of us. 'Meg does have a mummy but she doesn't see hers as much as you see yours.'

Isla nodded, but the two of them were quiet as I drove them back to the house, despite my attempts at conversation.

Meg was equally as dismissive when I introduced her to Louisa that night when she got home from work.

'She's been through a lot,' said Louisa sympathetically, once Meg had left the room.

'Yes, she's had a long day,' I replied. 'I think she just needs to sleep.'

To be fair, by early evening I was exhausted too. By the time I'd put Isla to bed at 7.30 p.m., I could hardly keep my eyes open.

'Time for bed, lovey,' I told Meg and she didn't put up any objections.

I didn't have to worry about how she was going to settle on her first night with us. Thankfully she was out like a light and I wasn't far behind her.

The following day Louisa dropped Isla at school for me again so I could let Meg sleep in. She finally emerged from her bedroom just after ten.

'You've had a good sleep.' I smiled. 'You obviously needed that.'

'Do I have to go to school?' she asked, bleary-eyed.

'Not today, lovey,' I told her. 'I think it will do you good just to have another quiet day here then you can go back to Mildred House tomorrow. Is that OK?'

She nodded.

I got on with some housework while Meg watched TV.

Just after lunch my mobile rang. It was Meg's social worker, Angela.

'How's she doing today?' she asked.

'She's fine,' I told her. 'She had a good night's sleep and she's not coughing as much as she was yesterday. I think she'll be fine to go to school tomorrow.'

'Good,' she said. 'There's something else I need to talk to you about. The police have just called me and they want to come round this afternoon and speak to Meg.'

'The police?' I asked, shocked. 'Why?'

'From their initial inquiries the fire brigade think the fire at Mildred House was started deliberately,' she said. 'They're interviewing all of the children and staff.'

'You mean they think it was arson?' I gasped. 'That's terrible.'

'It is,' agreed Angela. 'What kind of person would set fire to somewhere knowing there's children asleep inside?'

It was shocking.

'I'll let Meg know,' I told her. 'I've not mentioned the fire in case it was too traumatic for her. But if the police want to come round, then I'll sit with her while they speak to her.'

'Thanks, Maggie. It's just a formality in case she saw something that might help with their inquiries.'

I felt quite shaken when I came off the phone and I was worried about how Meg was going to take this news. I sat down on the sofa next to her and turned off the TV.

'Hey, I was watching that,' she huffed.

'I need to talk to you about something important,' I explained. 'That was Angela on the phone. The police want to come round and talk to you.'

Her face fell. 'The police?' she frowned. 'Why do they wanna talk to me?'

'They're talking to everyone who lived or worked at Mildred House to see if they know anything about the fire or how it might have started,' I explained. 'Just in case anyone saw anything strange or suspicious going on over the past few days.'

I didn't specifically say that they were treating it as arson as I felt that was better coming from the police.

I could see Meg was thinking deeply and suddenly her eyes became wide.

'I know something!' she gasped. 'Honestly, Maggie, I swear. I think somebody started the fire and I know who it was . . .'

THREE

Fireworks

'Are you sure about this, Meg?' I asked her, trying to keep the shock I was feeling out of my voice. 'That's a very serious thing to accuse someone of.'

'I swear I'm telling the truth,' she snapped. 'I think someone started the fire on purpose.'

I listened as she began to explain.

'There's this girl called Kayleigh,' she said breathlessly, fiddling with the hem of her T-shirt. 'She's always playing with lighters. She was in the garden the other day and I saw her setting fire to a pile of leaves. I told her we wasn't supposed to do that but she swore at me.'

'Did you tell anyone else about what you'd seen?' I asked.

Meg shook her head. 'She's older than me and I was scared she'd kick my head in if I grassed her up. If the police searched her stuff they'd find a lighter. I bet it was her that started the fire.'

Meg seemed very sure and it certainly sounded like something the police needed to look into, but I couldn't help but wonder why she hadn't said anything sooner. I put it down to her being overwhelmed after the stress of everything that had happened.

'When the police get here you need to tell them exactly what you've just told me,' I told her. 'OK?'

Meg nodded but I could see the worried look on her face.

'It's fine, I'll be with you,' I reassured her. 'They need to find out how the fire started and it's important that you tell them about this girl just in case it's connected.'

'But what if Kayleigh gets into trouble cos of me?' she asked, her eyes wide again.

'If someone did start the fire deliberately then the police need to know, lovey,' I told her. 'It's lucky that everyone got out safely but there's still been thousands of pounds worth of damage to the building. It's really serious, Meg. Any information you have needs to be passed on.'

'Alright,' she sighed, rolling her eyes. 'I get the message.'

Half an hour later there was a knock at the door. I opened it to find a female police officer on the doorstep. She looked like she was in her late forties and she had a friendly face and a warm smile.

'Gosh, that was quick,' I exclaimed. 'The social worker only phoned a little while ago to say you'd be coming.'

'We aim to be efficient.' She smiled, showing me her ID. 'I'm PC Trisha Hirst and I'm guessing you're Maggie? I'd like to speak to Meg, if that's OK?'

'Yes, come in,' I told her, leading her into the living room.

I needn't have worried. The PC had a calm, gentle manner and she couldn't have been nicer. However, Meg looked terrified as she walked in.

'I'm going to sit with Meg while you talk to her, if that's OK,' I said, after I'd got us all a cup of tea. 'She's been through a lot.'

'Yes, of course.' She nodded.

'How are you doing, Meg?' PC Hirst asked Meg gently. 'I was sorry to hear what happened yesterday. It must have been really scary for you. How are you feeling now?'

'OK,' she said meekly. 'My throat's still a bit sore.'

I could tell that she was nervous. She watched warily as PC Hirst got out her notebook.

'We're talking to everyone who was at Mildred House at the time of the fire to see if they saw anything unusual or whether they can remember anything that might help us with our inquiries,' PC Hirst explained. 'So, in your own time, please could you talk me through what happened?'

Meg looked at me apprehensively and I gave her a little nod of encouragement.

'Tell her what happened, lovey,' I urged her gently.

Meg coughed and then cleared her throat.

'I was in bed,' she began. 'I didn't know nothing was happening til Debbie our support worker came running in and woke us all up.'

'What did she say?' asked PC Hirst gently.

'She was shouting at us all to get out,' replied Meg. 'I didn't know what she was on about, but then I heard the fire alarms and I smelt it.'

'Smelt what?'

'The burning smell,' Meg sighed. 'When we ran into the corridor there was big clouds of smoke and we was all coughing and choking and I couldn't see nothing. We was all screaming and crying but Debbie managed to get us all out and then when I was outside on the grass I saw the orange flames coming out of the kitchen window.'

She stared off into the distance as if she was replaying the memory of that night in her head. Her eyes were all glassy and it looked as if she was about to cry.

'It was so hot,' she murmured. 'Even though I was outside I could still feel it stinging my face and my throat was burning.'

Her eyes were filled with tears and she looked very young all of a sudden.

I squeezed her hand to give her a bit of comfort and reassurance.

'Well done, Meg,' PC Hirst told her kindly. 'Thank you for going through all of that with me. It must have been really traumatic and you've been very brave.'

I looked over at Meg.

'Lovey, you need to tell PC Hirst what you were telling me this morning before she arrived.'

'Do I have to?' she sighed.

I nodded.

Hesitantly, Meg told her about Kayleigh and what had happened with the lighter.

PC Hirst took some notes.

'It probably don't even matter.' Meg shrugged when she'd finished.

'Well, actually it does matter, because at this stage the fire brigade think the fire at Mildred House was started deliberately,' PC Hirst explained in a serious voice.

'But why would someone do that?' asked Meg.

'That's exactly what we're trying to find out,' replied PC Hirst. 'So information like this is really crucial. But can I ask you why you think Kayleigh would set fire to the building and risk damaging her own things?'

'She ain't in our room,' Meg told her. 'She's over the other side of the building in another bedroom. Maybe she was pissed off I'd seen her with the lighter and she wanted to stop me from grassing her up so she set fire to our bit? Kind of like a warning for me to keep my mouth shut.

'You won't tell her, will you?' she added desperately, suddenly looking afraid. 'You won't say I told you about seeing her with the lighter?'

'Of course not,' said PC Hirst kindly. 'It's just one of a number of things that we'll be looking into, so don't worry.'

She closed her notebook.

'Well, thank you for going through everything with me, Meg, and if you remember anything else, no matter how small, let Maggie know and she can contact me,' she told her.

Meg nodded.

'I'll see you out.' I smiled.

'Do you think you'll look into the Kayleigh thing?' I asked, as I showed her to the front door.

'Oh definitely,' she said. 'We're following up any leads. The fire brigade believe the fire originated in the kitchen, possibly from some curtains being set alight so it could be that a lighter was used.'

As I shut the door, it still made me shudder to think someone had done this deliberately.

Meg was very quiet after PC Hirst had left. I could see that talking about the fire had left her shaken up so I made sure we had another quiet day.

In the afternoon her social worker Angela came round. I hadn't met her before but I warmed to her instantly. She was a tiny woman in her thirties with dark corkscrew curls and she was very pleasant and friendly.

'I thought I'd pop round and say hello and see how Meg is doing,' she told me.

'She's just watching TV,' I replied. 'I think the police visit wore her out.'

'Oh, how did it go?' she asked.

I explained about PC Hirst and what Meg had told her.

'Well, they'll certainly have to look into that,' she sighed.

I took her through to the living room where Meg was curled up on the sofa.

'Angela's here to see you,' I told her.

Meg looked up and frowned. 'What do you want?' she scowled, glaring at Angela.

'I just came to see how you were,' Angela replied, unfazed by Meg's rudeness. 'I was worried about you after the fire.'

She sat down on the end of the sofa next to her.

'Your mum was extremely worried about you too,' Angela continued. 'She was so upset to hear about the fire and that you'd been in hospital.'

She paused and gave me a look, and I sensed that she wasn't sure how this news was going to go down with Meg.

'In fact, Mum would really love to see you. I know it's been a little while and I wondered how you'd feel about me

112

organising a contact session in the next week or so? Sophie and Laura could come along too if you wanted?'

Meg sat up and glared at her. 'Why would I want to see them?' she spat. 'They don't care about me or the fire.'

'Meg, your mum was devastated about the fire,' Angela told her. 'She's desperate to see you and to check that you're OK.'

'Well, I don't want to see her,' Meg said defiantly.

'What about a phone call?' suggested Angela. 'If I gave her Maggie's number, would you talk to her if she rang?'

'I'll think about it,' she snapped, lying back down and staring at the TV.

It was clear that that conversation was over and done with. Angela and I went into the kitchen to chat.

'Well, that went down like a lead balloon,' she sighed.

'She's been through a lot and talking to the police really tired her out,' I told her. 'It might be worth asking her again in a few days. I'd be happy to have the contact session here if you think that would help?' I suggested.

'That's a good idea,' she said. 'It might make everything a bit more relaxed and less pressured. To be honest, I don't think anything is really going to change until Meg starts counselling to help her deal with her anger. I'll call CAMHS and chase it up this afternoon.' (CAMHS stands for the Child and Adolescent Mental Health Service and sadly they are always overstretched with long waiting lists.)

'In the meantime, perhaps in a few days I'll get Zoe, Meg's mum, to call you and you can put her on if she wants to speak to her?'

'That's absolutely fine,' I said.

We also had a chat about timescales.

'At this stage I don't have a definitive answer about how long Meg's going to be with you, I'm afraid,' Angela told me. 'There's a lot of damage to that side of the building at the children's home and the local authority is having to go through insurance before they can appoint contractors.'

'Honestly, it's fine,' I told her. 'I'm happy to have Meg as long as you need me to. Isla's probably only here for another couple of weeks so I have the space and, to be honest, she's been fine so far.'

'Thank you, Maggie,' said Angela. 'I really appreciate that.'

The following day Meg went back to Mildred House for lessons. A taxi came to pick her up that morning and dropped her back in the afternoon.

'How was it?' I asked her as she sloped back into the house.

'Same old boring lessons,' she sighed. 'It was weird seeing where my bedroom was before. It was black on the windows and it's all boarded up.'

'Did you see Kayleigh today?' I asked.

Meg nodded. 'But I didn't say nothing about the police.'

They'd managed to salvage some of the girls' things and Meg brought back a cardboard box with a few books and knick-knacks in it.

'They said the clothes were too smoky to keep,' she sighed.

'That doesn't matter because Social Services has given me an allowance to get you some new things,' I told her.

As the days passed, we settled into a new routine. Meg would go off in a taxi in the morning while I did the school run with Isla. Although Meg could be rude and snappy, I'd been expecting a lot worse with her behaviour. Angela phoned every few days and I chatted to her about it.

'Her behaviour was OK at the children's home too,' she told me. 'She had her moments and her fits of anger but nothing like what she was like when she was at home with Mum.'

With Meg giving Isla a wide berth, I wouldn't have said that they were friends, but at least there hadn't been any arguments.

Just over a week after she'd spoken to the police, Angela called with an update.

'PC Hirst phoned me today,' she told me. 'The fire investigation team have come to a bit of a dead end with their inquiries.'

She explained they were sure the fire at Mildred House had originated by the window in the kitchen and they suspected arson because there was nothing to suggest a fuse had tripped or that it was caused by an electrical fault.

'They didn't find evidence of any accelerants being used either,' she told me. 'So there's not a lot more they can do.'

'What about what Meg said about Kayleigh?' I asked. 'Did the police speak to her?'

'They did and she apparently denied being involved,' she sighed. 'She did have a lighter in her room but she said she used it for smoking and there's nothing that links her lighter to the fire. PC Hirst said in reality the only way they'd find out who had done it was if someone confessed.'

'That's hardly likely,' I said.

'Exactly,' she said. 'So they can't take it any further at this point in time.'

It was frustrating but there wasn't anything anyone could do.

*

A few weeks later it was Bonfire Night, and I'd arranged to take the girls to a fireworks display. It was a cold, frosty night so we all got wrapped up and traipsed to the local park.

'Can I do more sparklers?' asked Isla, jumping up and down with excitement.

'Sparklers are stupid,' huffed Meg, rolling her eyes.

'You've already gone through most of the packet so there's just one left.' I smiled, getting them out of my anorak pocket and ignoring Meg.

'Can I borrow your lighter again?' I asked Louisa.

I'd forgotten to bring a lighter or matches but her fiancé Charlie smoked and luckily she had his lighter in her handbag. Louisa flicked the top a few times but it didn't work. She tutted, gave it a shake and tried again.

'My mummy has one of those,' said Isla as she watched Louisa with the lighter. 'I love the way those sparkly things come out of the top. It's really pretty.'

'More like pretty useless,' groaned Louisa, frustrated.

Finally the lighter had a flame and Louisa managed to ignite the sparkler. Isla gave a squeal of excitement as she twirled it around and spelt out her name.

'Come on,' I told them when the sparkler had gone out and had been safely deposited into a nearby bucket of sand. 'Let's go and find a spot to watch the fireworks. They'll be starting in a minute.'

The event was packed and it was quite a squash as we squeezed our way through the hordes of people.

'You keep a firm hold of Isla and I'll keep an eye on Meg,' I told Louisa.

However, when I turned to speak to Meg, she wasn't behind me.

'Hang on!' I called to Louisa, my heart in my throat. 'I've lost Meg.'

She'd been there only a moment ago. We both looked around frantically, hoping to spot the pink bobble hat she was wearing in the crowd.

Nothing.

'You stay here with Isla while I go and look for her,' I told Louisa breathlessly.

My heart was pounding in my chest as I pushed through a sea of people. I knew she couldn't have gone far but I couldn't rest until I'd found her. I waited by the Portaloos in case she'd needed the loo, then looked by the snack vans where I thought she might have headed. I was starting to get really frantic when, to my relief, I spotted a familiar figure in a pink hat. She was standing by the bonfire, right up next to it on the front row, staring into the flames.

It was hard to read the look on her face. Was it fascination? Fear? Whatever it was, I could tell she was absolutely transfixed.

Then it suddenly hit me. What on earth was I thinking bringing her here tonight? Less than three weeks ago the poor child had been woken from her bed in the middle of the night by a fire. I remembered how upset she'd been talking to the police officer, describing how terrified she was seeing the flames, choking on the smoke and feeling the intense heat. And now I'd taken her to a massive bonfire.

I looked at Meg's face as she stared at the flames coming from the huge pile of dead wood. She was absolutely mesmerised. Had I traumatised the poor girl?

'Meg,' I called out, pushing my way through the crowd towards her. 'I thought we'd lost you.

'Are you OK, lovey?' I asked when I was level with her. 'I'm so sorry, it was a silly idea to bring you here. I don't know what I was thinking.'

'I was just watching the fire,' she said, not taking her eyes off it for a minute. 'The flames are really orange, aren't they. It's so hot, Maggie. I can feel it burning my face. When I was little, my mum used to take me and my sisters to a bonfire,' she added sadly. 'I used to love it. We'd do apple bobbing and have hot dogs when we got home.'

Her eyes were glassy and it seemed as though she was in a trance.

I had to get her away from there.

'Come on, flower, let's go and find Louisa and Isla and we can all get a hot chocolate and go back,' I said, ushering her away.

That night, as we walked home, I could have kicked myself for my insensitivity. There was going to be no more mention of fires at our house from now on.

FOUR

Up in Smoke

As I heard the home phone ring, my stomach knotted with nerves. I knew exactly who was at the other end and I was dreading how it was going to go down.

As I picked it up, I put it straight onto speakerphone.

'Hello, it's Maggie here,' I said loudly.

'Hi,' said a woman's voice hesitantly. 'It's–er Zoe. Meg's mum.'

Meg, who was sitting at the kitchen table doing her homework, froze when she heard her mother's voice.

'What does *she* want?' she sighed.

'Hello, Zoe,' I replied cheerfully. 'Meg's here in the kitchen with me. I'm just going to check on something in another room so I'll leave you two to chat.'

However, I lingered outside the kitchen door so I could hear what was being said between the two of them, just so I could step in if needed. Angela and I had talked about it and decided not to pre-warn Meg that her mum was calling so she didn't have the opportunity to kick off beforehand or disappear out of the room.

'Hi, Meg,' said Zoe cautiously. 'Angela said it would be OK to call you.'

'What do you want?' Meg huffed.

'I'm just checking on you to see if you're OK,' came Zoe's reply. 'I heard about the fire. That must have been so frightening for you.'

'Like you care,' muttered Meg.

'I do care,' she told her. 'I care a lot.'

There was an awkward silence.

'How's school going?' Zoe asked.

'Same as normal.'

'And what's it like at Maggie's?'

'Boring,' she snapped.

'What are you ringing for anyway?' Meg asked her suddenly. 'You don't care about me. You sent me away.'

'Oh, Meg, please don't do this again,' sighed Zoe. 'You do this every time.'

'Well, it's true,' Meg snapped.

'I'm going to arrange with Angela to come and see you,' Zoe pressed on. 'Your sisters would like to see you too.'

'I don't want you to come.'

'I'll talk to Maggie about it,' Zoe told her. 'Anyway, I have to go now because I have to pick up Laura from her afterschool club.'

'See, it's always about them, isn't it?' snapped Meg. 'Never about me. There ain't no point in you ringing.'

'You know that's not true,' said Zoe wearily. 'I have to pick Laura up because there's no one else to do it. I'm going to put the phone down now, Meg, but I'll speak to you soon, OK?'

I walked back into the room just in time to hear the dialling tone.

'Can you hear that?' shouted Meg. 'The silly bitch hung up on me! She's such a f*****g liar. She don't care about me. She don't wanna see me really.'

'Meg, I know you're upset but mind your language,' I told her firmly. 'I don't want to hear that kind of language in this house.'

'Don't tell me what to do,' yelled Meg. 'I'll say whatever the f**k I want.'

With that, she got up from the table, stormed out of the kitchen and slammed the door.

'Well, that sounded like it went well,' said Louisa grimly as she came into the kitchen.

'She and her mum just seem to wind each other up,' I sighed. 'She's been fine most of the time she's been here but any mention of Mum and she gets so, so angry.'

I would report what had happened to Angela but after hearing Meg's outburst on the phone, I wasn't sure it was even worth trying to set up a contact session.

I let Meg calm down for a while and fifteen minutes later I went up to her bedroom to check on her. I knocked on the door and when I went in, she was curled up on the bed. I could tell by her red eyes that she'd been crying.

'Are you OK, lovey?' I asked gently, sitting down on the bed next to her. 'You got very angry with your mum.'

I paused.

'Do you think that's because you miss her?'

'No!' she snapped.

Then she looked down at the floor.

'Maybe a bit,' she sighed sadly, her bottom lip trembling. 'I didn't mean to be nasty to her. But when I talk to her it makes me feel sad about what happened and how she put me in care and then I get really, really cross.'

She was only twelve and I could see she was struggling to process her feelings.

'We all feel angry sometimes, flower,' I told her gently. 'That's normal. Hopefully soon Angela will arrange for you to speak to someone who can try to help you feel less angry.'

'Will it stop me being horrible?' she asked.

As she spoke, looking up at me with her big dark eyes, I was reminded again that she was still just a little girl.

'It won't stop you,' I explained. 'Only you can control how you behave when you're feeling cross or upset. But there are people who can suggest things you can try when you do feel really angry. Things that you can do that will help you calm down and not be so cross.'

'Can I speak to them people soon?' she asked hopefully.

'I hope so, lovey,' I told her.

The sooner Meg had some counselling, the better, as far as I was concerned.

The following evening when Louisa got in from work, she asked to have a quick word with me. I was in the middle of making the girls' tea but I noticed the worried look on her face.

'Of course, lovey,' I told her. 'Give me two minutes.'

I quickly dished up the fish fingers then followed her into the front room.

'Whatever's the matter, flower?' I asked anxiously. 'Is Charlie OK? Is everything alright at work?'

'Yeah, everything's fine, don't worry,' she reassured me. 'It's probably nothing but I thought I'd better mention it to you.'

I was really intrigued now.

'Charlie put his cigarettes and lighter in my bag when we were out last night like he always does,' she explained. 'But when I met him at lunchtime I went to give them back to him and the cigarettes were there but the lighter wasn't.'

'What do you mean it wasn't there?' I asked, puzzled. 'Do you think you've lost it?'

'I don't see how I can have,' sighed Louisa. 'I know it was still in my bag at the end of the night as I saw it when I was getting out my car keys. I came straight home and I went to work as normal this morning.'

'Have you checked your car in case it dropped out?' I asked.

'Yep.' Louisa nodded. 'And I've just searched my room and there's no sign of the lighter anywhere.'

She paused.

'It's probably nothing but I thought I'd better tell you just in case,' she added.

'Just in case what?' I frowned.

'Just in case someone has taken it.'

I looked at Louisa and I knew exactly what she was thinking.

'I know it sounds silly,' she told me. 'But I can't stop thinking about last week at the bonfire when I was lighting the sparkler for Isla.'

'And she said how much she loved the lighter and how her mummy had one,' I interrupted. 'Yes, I remember.'

'She said she liked the sparkly bits that came out of the top when you flicked it,' Louisa went on. 'Do you really think she could have taken it out of my bag, Maggie?'

I shrugged.

'It could be that she's missing her mum more than we thought,' I sighed. 'I'll have a chat to her about it and ask her. I'm sure there's an innocent explanation and the lighter will turn up.'

I knew that was probably the case, but naturally I needed to make sure. I couldn't risk a child having a lighter in their possession.

That night when I went to tuck Isla into bed, I mentioned that Charlie's lighter had gone missing from Louisa's bag.

'I just wondered if perhaps you'd seen it?' I asked casually. 'Maybe it dropped out and you found it on the floor or you took it by mistake?'

She shook her head, frowning.

'I haven't got it,' she said.

'I wouldn't be cross with you if you had, you know, flower,' I told her. 'Lighters are very dangerous things so I just want to make sure it's in a safe place.'

'I promise, Maggie, I haven't taken it,' she said, tears pricking her eyes. 'I'm not telling fibs. I haven't seen it.'

'It's OK, sweetie, there's no need to get upset,' I soothed, brushing her tears away with my hand. 'I'm going to talk to Meg too. I just want to find it.'

Meg was downstairs watching TV.

'Nope,' she said when I asked her. 'I ain't seen it.'

'Are you sure?' I asked.

'What, you think I've nicked it?' she snapped.

'No, I didn't say that,' I told her patiently. 'I was just worried in case it had got into the wrong hands.'

'I swear I ain't taken any lighter,' she said. 'You told me not to go into Louisa's room.'

With that, she turned her attention back to her programme.

I didn't know what to make of it, but I told Louisa what both of them had said.

'There's not a lot more we can do,' I said to her. 'I'm sure there's an innocent explanation and it will turn up in a day or two.'

'Yeah you're probably right,' she sighed. 'Sorry, Maggie, I was just a bit worried one of the girls had got it.'

'No, you did the right thing mentioning it to me, lovey.' I smiled. 'Always better to be safe than sorry.'

The following day, while the girls were at school, Angela rang me.

'I know the phone call between Meg and her mum didn't go very well,' she said, 'but Zoe keeps asking me about contact. She thinks seeing Meg face to face might be better for both of them, so I thought it might be worth you mentioning it to Meg to test the water and see what she thinks.'

'I can try,' I told her. 'Although after the other day I'm not sure how it will go down.'

'Maybe if you say it can be at your house then that will make a difference?' she suggested.

'OK,' I agreed. 'I'll speak to Meg and let you know.'

When Meg got home from school that night, I had a drink and snack waiting for her. Isla was playing upstairs in her bedroom so it gave me a chance to talk to her alone.

'I was chatting to Angela today,' I told her as I loaded up the dishwasher. 'She mentioned how much your mum would really like to see you.'

Meg didn't say a word and kept on eating her crisps.

'Instead of the contact centre, I was thinking maybe you'd like your mum to come here?' I asked. 'You could show her your room and have a chat. She could bring your sisters too if you wanted her to? It's up to you. What do you think?'

I looked up at Meg. She crunched loudly on her last crisp, pushed her chair back from the table and stood up.

'How many times do I have to tell you people I don't wanna see her?' she yelled, scrunching up her crisp packet and throwing it on the floor. 'There ain't no point. She put me in care. She hates me and my stupid sisters hate me, so I don't know why she's pretending. I don't care if I don't ever see them again and I don't want them here.'

'It's OK, Meg,' I soothed, trying to calm her down. 'You don't have to see them if you don't want to. It was just an idea.'

'It was a stupid f*****g idea,' she yelled.

I could see her shoulders were shaking. I wasn't sure whether it was with rage or upset.

'Meg, please sit back down and take some deep breaths,' I told her.

I went to the sink and got her some water.

'Have a sip of this,' I told her, gently putting my hand on her shoulder.

'Just get off me and leave me alone,' she snapped, shrugging my hand off and turning her head away.

I'd got the message.

'I'm going to go upstairs to check on Isla,' I told her. 'Finish your drink and when you've calmed down, come and join us.'

I went upstairs to find Isla happily playing with the doll's house in her bedroom.

'Can I join in?' I asked her.

I wanted to give Meg a bit of breathing space after her outburst.

'Yes.' Isla smiled. 'You can be the daddy.'

It was a nice escape for a while, lying on the carpet playing dolls while Meg cooled off downstairs. Around fifteen minutes later I heard her stomp up the stairs and her bedroom door slam shut.

'What's wrong with Meg?' asked Isla. 'Why's she so cross all the time?'

'I think sometimes she feels a bit sad,' I told her.

'Anyway.' I smiled, deflecting the conversation back to the dolls. 'What should the daddy doll make for dinner?'

'Sausages and chips,' Isla grinned.

As I lay on the carpet. I glanced out of Isla's bedroom window and noticed an orange glow in the sky. It was just after 4 p.m. and now that we were in November, it was starting to get dark already, and it looked like it was the beginning of a lovely sunset.

I heaved myself up off the floor and went over to the window to look out at the sky. But as I looked through the glass, I stopped dead in my tracks. The orange glow wasn't coming from the sun. It was coming from the shed at the bottom of my garden.

Isla came running over to the window and let out a high-pitched scream.

'Maggie, Maggie!' she yelled. 'The garden's on fire.'

The wooden shed was completely ablaze. Thick black plumes of smoke rose high into the air and vivid orange flames licked at the windows. But worse still, I could see the fire had already spread to one side of the wooden fence and the flames were edging up the garden towards my house.

I knew then that I needed to get the girls out of the house as quickly as possible.

'Isla, quick, come on,' I said breathlessly. 'We need to get out.'

Isla looked at me, her big blue eyes filled with fear.

'I can smell burning,' she gasped. 'Is it going to burn us, Maggie?'

I didn't dare answer, but grabbed her hand and ran out onto the landing, Isla close behind.

'Meg!' I screamed. 'Meg! We need to get out now!'

Meg's bedroom was at the front of the house so she wouldn't have seen the fire.

'What?' I heard her shout.

I ran to her bedroom door and pounded on it.

'Meg, there's a fire in the back garden, it's heading towards the house and we need to get out now,' I urged her.

'What are you talking about?' she said, opening the door. 'Why do we need to get out?'

'There's no time for questions, Meg, we need to go right now,' I said firmly.

My heart was hammering in my chest as the girls and I ran down the stairs. I knew the safest thing would be to get them out at the front of the house, well away from the fire at the back.

'Stay here,' I told them firmly, once we were safely in the front drive.

Poor Isla was in tears and she looked terrified.

'I'm scared, Maggie,' she wept. 'What if the fire burns us?'

'It's going to be OK, flower,' I promised her. 'It's not going to come here. We're all going to be fine.

'You stay with Meg. She'll look after you and I'll be back in a minute.'

I ran back into the house and grabbed my mobile off the side in the hallway. My hands were shaking as I quickly dialled 999.

'Fire brigade,' I told the operator.

As soon as I got through to someone I gave them my address.

'We've already received another call from a neighbour about this blaze,' she explained. 'There's a unit on its way.'

It can't get here soon enough, I thought anxiously as I ran into the kitchen. The fire had completely engulfed the shed and was edging its way along the fence. It was now dangerously close to the house.

I unlocked the patio doors and ran out into the garden to see if I could spray the hose on it, but I quickly realised that it would be far too dangerous. The heat was so intense and it was like nothing I'd ever felt before. Soon I was engulfed in clouds of black smoke and it made my throat smart.

'Maggie!' I heard a voice yell over the side of the fence that wasn't ablaze. 'Are you OK?'

It was my neighbour, Steve.

'Yes,' I coughed. 'The girls are out the front and the fire brigade's on its way.'

'Thank God,' he exclaimed. 'I saw the smoke out of the window and phoned 999. You should go out to the front too, Maggie. It's moving fast.'

He was right. My whole body was tensed with fear as I saw the flames edging nearer and nearer to my beloved house. What would I do if the fire destroyed my home?

Hurry up, I thought desperately, willing the fire brigade to arrive.

'Maggie, get yourself out of there!' Steve yelled from the other side of the fence. 'It's too dangerous!'

He was right. The fire was dangerously close now.

I turned and was about to go back inside when I felt something crunch underneath my foot. I looked down and picked up the object that I'd stood on.

A plastic lighter.

My stomach lurched, as a terrible thought crossed my mind. But I didn't have time to stop and think.

I shoved the lighter into my pocket and ran to safety.

FIVE

Hidden Truths

As I ran through the house, I was relieved to hear the sirens approaching in the distance. The girls were still standing outside the front and Steve's wife Wendy had kindly wrapped them in a blanket each and given them a drink of water. Isla, bless her, was still crying.

'Maggie, you're alive!' she sobbed as she saw me run down the front path towards her.

'Of course I am, silly.' I smiled, giving her a reassuring cuddle. 'It's going to be OK, the fire brigade are here now. They'll put the fire out.'

I watched gratefully as the fire engine screeched to a halt outside and a team of firefighters raced into action, dragging a hose through to the back.

'It's the shed and the fence in the back garden that's on fire,' I told them urgently, silently praying that the flames hadn't reached the back of the house.

I looked over at Meg and realised she hadn't said a word since leaving the house. I was all too aware that this was the second fire that she'd been involved in in just over a month.

'Are you OK, flower?' I asked her gently, my hand on her shoulder. I couldn't imagine how frightening it must be for her to be involved in another fire so soon after the one that had destroyed almost all of her possessions.

She nodded. She was glassy-eyed and shaking with cold, despite the blanket.

Ten minutes later one of the firefighters came out to see me.

'We've managed to get it under control,' he said. 'The shed has been completely destroyed as has the right-hand side of the fence.

'There's a bit of smoke damage to the back wall of the house but nothing too serious. We got to it in the nick of time.'

'Oh, thank goodness,' I sighed, knowing it could have been so much worse.

'Are you all OK?' he asked, gesturing to me and the girls. 'Do you need to go to the hospital?'

'We're fine, thank you. Just a bit shaken up,' I told him. 'Thankfully I spotted it quite early on and we all got out pretty quickly. Have you got any idea how it might have started?' I asked him.

'At this stage, no,' he said. 'The fire investigation team will have a look when everything has cooled down. Do you have electricity in the shed?'

I shook my head. I didn't keep anything electrical in there either. I didn't even have a lawnmower as it had broken a few weeks ago and I'd taken it to the tip. It was mainly full of toys for the garden and my wooden table and chairs.

As the fire brigade packed away their equipment, I ran over the sequence of events in my mind.

I was talking to Meg about her mum. She got angry. I came upstairs to play with Isla.

She was the only person downstairs at the time. Ten minutes later I'd heard her storm up the stairs and then I'd spotted the smoke.

My hand went to my pocket and I felt the outline of the lighter.

Charlie's missing lighter.

It was then that the awful truth dawned on me.

My stomach was in knots as I quickly pulled Meg to one side, out of earshot of Isla, Wendy and Steve.

'It was you, wasn't it?' I asked her, trying hard to keep my voice steady.

'Tell me the truth, Meg,' I said firmly. 'You set fire to the shed, didn't you?'

'No, I never,' muttered Meg, looking at the ground.

'Look me in the eye and tell me it wasn't you,' I urged her. She couldn't.

That was all the confirmation I needed.

I felt sick as I stared down at the young girl.

'Why?' I gasped, horrified. 'Why would you do that, Meg? You could have hurt us. In fact, you could have killed us. The whole house could have gone up. What on earth were you thinking?'

She started to cry.

'I was so angry about my mum,' she sniffled. 'I didn't know what to do.'

'Did you take Charlie's lighter from Louisa's bag?' I asked her, scarcely able to believe what I was hearing.

She nodded sheepishly.

'You asked me to take some washing in there the other day and put it on her bed and I saw it sticking out her bag when she was in the shower. I didn't mean to hurt anyone,' she sobbed. 'I weren't thinking. Please don't tell anyone, Maggie. I'm sorry. I promise I won't do anything like that ever again.'

'I have to, Meg,' I told her firmly. 'I can't keep something this serious to myself. You put all of us in danger.'

I walked over to the firefighter who had spoken to me before.

'I need to give you this,' I said grimly, delving into my pocket and handing him the broken lighter. 'I found it in the garden just after the fire.

'And I'm afraid I know how it started. Meg over there has just confessed to me that she was the one who started the fire with this lighter.'

He stared at the lighter in my hand and then over at Meg, who was standing looking terrified, huddled under the blanket.

'Right,' he said. 'I see.'

'What happens now?' I asked nervously.

'When I get back to the office I'll have to fill in a report,' he said. 'If it's arson then I'll have to pass it straight on to the police. They'll want to speak to the young lady involved.'

'I'm so sorry,' I sighed. 'I had no idea she was going to do this.'

'I'm just glad everyone's OK,' he said, smiling sympathetically.

As the fire engine pulled away, my mind was reeling. I think I was in shock after the fire and I couldn't begin to process what Meg had just told me.

'Do you want to come into our house for a bit?' asked Steve kindly. 'Wendy will put the kettle on.'

'No, thank you,' I told him shakily. 'We'll be fine. I need to phone the girls' social workers and also assess how much damage there is.'

Isla clung onto my hand as we cautiously walked through to the kitchen. The poor little mite still looked terrified. The patio doors were wide open and the smell of acrid smoke hung in the air.

'The garden's all black,' gasped Isla, looking through the kitchen window.

The shed had been reduced to a pile of blackened wood that was still smoking and the fence had all but collapsed. The brickwork at the back of the house was singed and I shuddered when I saw how close it had got to the UPVC patio doors.

I wanted to cry as I looked at the damage, but I knew I had to hold myself together for the girls' sakes.

Meg sat quietly at the kitchen table. I was absolutely livid with her for putting us all at risk like that. As tempting as it was, I knew shouting and screaming wouldn't be helpful for anyone, so I took a few deep breaths to try and calm myself down.

'Do you want me to go to my room?' she asked sheepishly.

'No. I want you to stay right where I can see you,' I told her firmly.

My head was reeling and I wasn't sure what to do next. Thankfully, just then I heard Louisa's key in the front door. Her face fell when she walked through to the kitchen and saw the blackened shell that remained of the garden.

'What on earth has happened here?' she gasped.

'There was a big fire,' Isla told her. 'We had to run out and a fire engine came and everything.'

Louisa looked at me, astonished.

'There was a fire in the shed,' I explained wearily. 'We got out very quickly. We're all OK, although the garden has seen better days.'

'You should have rung me, Maggie,' she exclaimed, looking stricken.

'We've not been back in the house long,' I told her. 'The fire brigade has only just gone.'

'How on earth did it happen?' she asked.

Meg buried her head in her hands and I pulled Louisa to one side.

'Meg confessed to me that she did it,' I told her quietly. 'She admitted taking Charlie's lighter from your bag and using it to set fire to the shed.'

'What?' she gasped. 'But why on earth would she want to start a fire?'

'She was angry about her mum,' I sighed. 'I was trying to arrange a contact session.'

Louisa looked as shocked as I was.

'Will you stay with the girls for ten minutes while I go upstairs and make a few calls to my agency and their social workers?'

'Yes, of course.' She nodded. 'I'm so sorry about the lighter, Maggie.'

'It's not your fault at all, lovey,' I reassured her. 'You did the right thing telling me about it in the first place. Clearly you were right to be concerned.'

I grabbed my mobile and went up to my bedroom. I gave Becky a ring first. She was my supervising social worker at the fostering agency I worked for and therefore my first port of call. I explained what had happened.

'Blimey, Maggie,' she sighed after I'd filled her in. 'I'm so glad you're all OK. Is the house badly damaged or are you able to stay there?'

'It's fine,' I told her. 'It's just the garden that's damaged, but we can do without that for now given that it's winter.'

'I'll phone Isla's social worker and let her know what's happened,' replied Becky.

'Thank you,' I said. 'But there's something else I need to talk to you about, Becky.'

I told her about Meg's confession.

'What on earth was she thinking, Maggie?' she gasped when I'd finished.

'God only knows,' I sighed. 'I'll phone Angela, Meg's social worker after we've finished. And I expect the police will want to interview Meg at some point too.'

Because of what had happened, Becky had to do a risk assessment.

'How do you feel about keeping Meg with you tonight?' she asked. 'Do you think she could try it again?'

'My gut instinct is telling me no,' I sighed. 'She's been here five weeks and this is the first time that anything like this has happened. I think it was a one-off, a moment of madness when she was angry with her mum.'

'OK,' said Becky. 'I'd advise you to search her room just to check she doesn't have any lighters or matches or anything else that could possibly be used to start a fire. And, Maggie, please ring me or the overnight duty social worker if anything else happens or you're concerned about anything,' she added.

'I will do,' I replied.

'Maggie, you know I have to ask this,' she said.

'Yes?' I asked.

'You don't think that Meg could have had anything to do with the fire at the children's home?'

I felt a sinking feeling in the pit of my stomach as Becky voiced the concern that had been in the back of my mind ever since Meg's confession. But I quickly dismissed it.

'No,' I replied firmly. 'No way. The shed fire was a silly, spur of the moment thing. There's no way she would have set fire to an entire building with people inside. She's only twelve, she's not that malicious.'

'You're right,' sighed Becky. 'I felt like I had to ask. Just ignore me. I'm putting two and two together and getting five.'

I didn't blame Becky for asking the question. The thought had fleetingly crossed my mind when I'd found the lighter, but deep down I knew there was no way that Meg was capable of something on that scale. The fire at Mildred House was in a different league to a small blaze in a shed started in a fit of childish anger.

After I put down the phone to Becky, I dialled Angela's number. She was equally as shocked and horrified by the day's events as Becky had been. I went through everything again with her and told her about searching Meg's bedroom to check it was safe.

'I keep anything like matches and lighters locked away but she could have brought something back from the children's home,' I told her. 'So I need to be sure that Isla and Louisa aren't at risk.'

'Absolutely,' she agreed. 'I'll be round first thing in the morning to talk to her.'

When I came downstairs, Louisa had made the girls some beans on toast.

'Oh you're an angel.' I smiled.

'I thought the least I could do to help was give them tea,' she said.

As the girls tucked into their meal, I turned to Meg.

'I'll be searching your room in a minute, Meg. I can't risk you having lighters or anything that could start a fire in there,' I told her. 'I'd like you to come upstairs when you've finished tea, please.'

'But I don't want you to,' she snapped. 'I told you I ain't got any more lighters up there.'

'If you want to stay in this house tonight then I have to,' I told her firmly. 'The other alternative is that I give Angela a ring and she will find you another foster carer to go to tonight.'

Meg didn't say a word but sat with her arms folded, scowling.

The other thing that I would have to do tonight was to put the house in lockdown, meaning that the doors to most of the rooms would be locked when we weren't in them. That way, Meg wouldn't be able to go into the kitchen, the living room or anyone else's bedroom on her own. It was a real pain for everyone constantly having to lock and unlock doors, but under the circumstances, I felt that it was the only way to make sure that we stayed safe.

I went upstairs into Meg's bedroom. She had brought so little with her that there wasn't much to search through. I went through her chest of drawers first, making sure I felt every item of clothing and pair of socks and pulling each drawer out. There was nothing at the bottom of the wardrobe or in her bedside table or under the rug. Finally I decided to pull her bed away from the wall just in case she'd stuffed something down the side of it. As I pulled out the bed, I gasped in shock. All along the skirting board was a line of small burn marks. Not enough to set off a smoke alarm or make a noticeable smell, but there was at least twenty places where the wood had been scorched.

I searched her bed next. My heart thumped as I felt a carrier bag tucked under the mattress. I opened it up to find a couple of lighters, a box of matches and several scraps of burnt paper.

I felt sick. The shed fire clearly hadn't been the one-off moment of madness that Meg had claimed.

'Meg!' I called down the stairs. 'Can you come up here now, please.'

I heard her footsteps stomping up the stairs.

'What is it?' she frowned.

I gestured to the line of burn marks and the carrier bag and her face fell.

'What can you tell me about these?' I asked.

'I . . . er . . .' she mumbled.

I was furious with her. Furious that she had put herself, Isla, Louisa and me in danger. Furious that she had been hiding this fire-starting kit right under our noses.

Suddenly, everything became clear. I felt sick to my stomach as the truth dawned on me, but I knew I had to say the words that I was thinking in my head aloud.

'It was you, Meg, wasn't it?' I asked. 'It was you who started the fire at Mildred House.'

She looked up at me, her brown eyes filled with fear, and then she nodded.

'Yes,' she whispered. 'It was me.'

SIX

Coming Clean

I felt sick to my stomach. Setting fire to a rickety garden shed was one thing, but a children's home with people inside it was on another level entirely. I had truly never thought that she was capable of doing such a thing, and I was horrified.

Meg sank down onto the bed and curled up into a ball.

'You can't tell on me, Maggie,' she sobbed, rocking backwards and forwards. 'You can't tell anyone.'

'They'll put me in prison.'

I was shocked and angry at what she'd done, but there was also a part of me that was desperately sad. Sad that she felt so much pain and anger that she had had to resort to releasing it in such a destructive way, and sad that the system had somehow let her down. If she'd been able to have therapy instead of languishing on a waiting list for months, this might never have happened.

I sat down beside her on the bed. I needed to try and put emotion to one side and get the facts.

'Did you start the fire at Mildred House with a lighter, Meg?' I asked her, trying to keep my voice calm and steady.

Meg shook her head.

'I couldn't sleep and I went into the kitchen to get a drink,' she said. 'I was thinking about my mum and how she would get me a drink and a piece of toast sometimes if I couldn't sleep. I don't know why but I put the edge of the curtain on the hob and switched the heat on, just to see what would happen.'

Tears ran down her face.

'I didn't mean it, Maggie,' she sobbed. 'I didn't know it would go up so quickly. I tried to put it out but I couldn't. I was really scared, so I ran back to bed.'

I couldn't believe that she had behaved so thoughtlessly, and I shuddered as I thought about the danger she had put herself and the other children in.

'Why?' I asked, sighing heavily. 'What on earth made you do it?'

She shrugged.

'It makes me feel better,' she mumbled. 'I like the way it smells and how warm the flames get. It stops me feeling sad.'

I remembered Bonfire Night and how I couldn't drag her away from the fire. I'd thought it was fear but in fact it was fascination. Starting a fire was an outlet for her.

'Why did you accuse Kayleigh?' I asked.

She looked down at the floor, looking guilty.

'I was scared what would happen if they knew it was me. I'd seen Kayleigh with a lighter when she was smoking and I thought it would stop them blaming me. Please don't tell,' she begged, her brown eyes wide with fear.

'I have to, Meg,' I sighed. 'This is so serious. You could have killed someone, including yourself.'

'I–I–I didn't m–mean it,' she wept, hardly able to get the words out.

I looked at her sitting on the bed, her body shaking with sobs and my heart went out to her. Despite the terrible thing she'd done, she looked so vulnerable and broken.

'You hate me, don't you?' she whimpered. 'You hate me just like my mum does.'

'I don't hate you, flower,' I replied. 'And neither does your mum. I don't like what you've done but I can see how much pain you're in and I want to try and make things better for you. Whatever happens, Meg, I'll be there for you,' I promised her. 'We'll face this together but you have to tell the truth.'

I put my arm around her and she buried her face in my shoulder and cried it out. Eventually she went quiet and I felt her body go limp in my arms. I could see she was exhausted.

'I'm going to go downstairs now to make a few phone calls,' I told her gently. 'I want you to come downstairs and sit with Louisa and Isla.'

She shook her head.

'No, I want to stay here,' she whimpered. 'I don't want to see them.'

'Meg, after everything that you've just told me I don't want to risk leaving you on your own,' I told her firmly.

I led her downstairs to the living room where Isla was sitting with Louisa watching the TV. I took Louisa to one side and explained what had happened. All the colour drained from her face.

'The silly girl,' she sighed.

'I know,' I replied. 'I can't believe it.'

I phoned my agency first. Becky had gone home so I spoke to Kate, one of the duty social workers.

'I'll phone Meg's social worker now,' I told her. 'We'll work out which one of us will call the police.'

'Do you feel able to have Meg in the house tonight?' asked Kate. 'Do you think it's a risk to your other placement?'

'I've searched her room and removed all the matches and lighters and I'll lock all the communal areas so Meg won't have access to them without me being present,' I told her. 'We can manage tonight, then we'll have to reassess in the morning.'

I didn't think Meg would attempt to start a fire again now that we knew the truth but I couldn't assume anything. I knew that I would be watching her every move like a hawk.

My next phone call was to Angela.

'She did what?' she gasped.

She was absolutely devastated.

'Even when you told me about the fire in your garden earlier, it never even crossed my mind that she could be responsible for what happened at Mildred House. We need to let the police know ASAP,' she told me. 'I'll call PC Hirst and let you know what's going to happen.'

A few minutes later, Angela rang back to say the police wanted Meg to go to the station the next day to make a statement.

'I'll phone Zoe and let her know, then I'll arrange for a solicitor to go to the police station tomorrow,' she told me. 'I'm happy to go with Meg as I know you'll have Isla.'

I'd assured Meg that I'd be there for her and I knew I had to keep that promise.

'Thanks, Angela, but I'll go with Meg,' I told her. 'Hopefully Louisa can have Isla after school, but if not then I'm sure my friend Vicky will help.'

Once I'd finished making the necessary calls, I took Meg upstairs to tell her what had happened. She looked very young as she climbed onto her bed and curled up in a ball.

'Did you do it?' she whispered, her pale face streaked with tears. 'Did you tell them?'

'You know I had to tell them, Meg,' I told her gently. 'We're going to need to go down to the police station tomorrow afternoon.'

'Will they lock me up?' she sobbed. 'Am I going to prison?'

I felt that under these circumstances, I owed it to her to be truthful.

'To be honest, Meg, I don't know,' I sighed. 'Children don't go to prison, they go to secure units, but there's no point worrying about it now. What I want you to do is have a bath and get in your pyjamas while I put Isla to bed.'

'You won't tell Isla, will you?' she begged.

'No, lovey. I don't want to scare her,' I said.

Forty minutes later when Isla was tucked up in bed, I went to check on Meg. She was lying on the bed fast asleep. I gently pulled her duvet over her. I was still absolutely furious with her for what she'd done but deep down there was a part of me that understood why she'd done it. With my professional head on, I knew it had come from a place of anger and fear, and an inability to express her feelings of abandonment and hurt. She looked so young and fragile lying there fast asleep. I knew she was physically and emotionally exhausted after all the drama and I was too. I still felt in shock as I quietly tiptoed out of the room.

'What a day,' I sighed to Louisa, when I went downstairs. 'I can't get over everything's that happened.'

'I don't understand why she did it.' Louisa frowned. 'Why would you set fire to something?'

'I know it's hard to understand but it's not as rare as you think,' I told her.

I'd been on a training course where we had talked about children who started fires.

'There are all different sorts of reasons,' I explained. 'It can be boredom or sometimes they want attention or even that they enjoy the anticipation of being caught. Starting a fire gives them a high.'

In Meg's case I felt that it was an outlet. It was a way for her to express her anger and hurt about being put into care.

Before I went to bed, I locked the kitchen and the front room. I hated it when I had to put the house in lockdown but there was no choice – I couldn't risk Meg being on her own in the kitchen with all the electrics and the hob and other potential fire risks.

Even though I was exhausted, I lay in bed that night unable to sleep. My head was spinning and every tiny noise or creak of a floorboard made me sit bolt upright in bed, worried that Meg was up to something. By the time it got light the following morning, I'd hardly slept a wink.

At breakfast Meg was extremely quiet.

'Do I have to go to school?' she eventually asked.

'I think you should,' I said. 'We're not due at the police station until four o'clock so let's try and keep things as normal as possible.'

'But do they know at Mildred House what I did?' she asked. 'They ain't gonna want me there if they know I was the one who started the fire.'

'The staff might but the other children won't,' I reassured her.

Once Meg had gone off in the taxi, I took Isla to school as normal. It felt strange to be back in our familiar routine after everything that had happened. But as soon as I got home, my mobile rang. It was Becky.

'Oh, Maggie,' she sighed when I answered. 'I've just heard about Meg's confession.'

'I know,' I sighed. 'Your suspicions were right. I'm still trying to get my head around it all. I can hardly believe it.'

She explained that she and Angela were on their way over to my house.

When they'd both arrived, I made us all a coffee and we sat around the kitchen table.

'Your garden's a mess,' sighed Angela, looking out through the patio doors at the blackened grass.

'That's the least of my worries.' I smiled wryly. 'I'm just glad the fire didn't get as far as the house.'

Becky's main concern as my supervising social worker was Isla.

'After everything that's happened I don't feel that it's safe to have another child in the house with Meg,' said Becky.

'But where would Meg go?' I asked.

Angela shrugged.

'I know there are no children's home places locally,' she said. 'The only option would be to move her to another carer but it would have to be someone who wasn't fostering anyone else.'

'She's going to find it really hard being moved again,' I sighed.

I still felt incredibly angry about what she'd done but in my heart I knew she needed my help, not my judgement. She was confused, and at twelve, just a child who needed my support.

She was already struggling to cope with being rejected by her mother and she was terrified of what was going to happen with the police. I'd promised to be there for her.

'Does it have to be Meg that goes?' I asked quietly.

I couldn't believe I was suggesting that it was Isla who left. Sweet little Isla, who had never given me a moment's trouble in all the time she'd been here.

'Well, she was due to go in a couple of weeks anyway,' said Becky. 'I spoke to her mum Agnes yesterday and she's doing much better than she thought she would be. She's out of hospital now and they've got her back up and on her feet much faster than she was expecting. I could talk to her and suggest that perhaps Isla could go back home?'

'What, now?' I asked, shocked.

'I think Agnes would need a bit more notice than that, but maybe we could try for tomorrow?'

I had always known that Isla would be going home at some point, but it was still a shock that it could be so soon.

Once Becky and Angela had left, I did what I always did at times when I was feeling upset or down: I embarked on a cleaning spree. But as I scrubbed the kitchen from top to bottom, it did nothing to take away the pang of sadness I was feeling in the pit of my stomach when I thought about sweet little Isla and how much I was going to miss having her around.

Later that day, Becky called me and confirmed that Agnes was sure she could cope with having Isla home with her again.

'She sounded delighted to be getting her daughter back early,' she told me.

On the walk back from school I told Isla the news. I put on my best cheerful voice despite the fact that inside, my heart was heavy with sadness.

'Guess what?' I told her. 'Since you last saw her, your mummy's come home from hospital and she's feeling much better. The doctors are really pleased and she's walking around again so the good news is you can go home.'

'Home?' she gasped, her blue eyes sparkling with delight. 'To Mummy?'

'Yes.' I smiled. 'Isn't that brilliant?'

Isla nodded and she had the biggest grin on her face.

'Will you help me pack my things?' she asked excitedly. 'I can be ready super quickly.'

'I will help you pack, lovey, but you're not going home until tomorrow after school,' I said.

Isla looked disappointed.

'Your mummy needs a bit of time to make sure everything is sorted out at home and all ready for you,' I explained.

The guilt I'd been feeling all day at choosing Meg over Isla lifted slightly at the thought that Isla was so excited to be going home.

But there were other things on my mind, too. Louisa had arranged to come home early so she could look after Isla while I took Meg to the police station.

I could tell Meg was absolutely dreading it.

'Do we have to go?' she asked, looking terrified.

'Yes, sweetie,' I told her. 'The police are expecting you.'

When we got to the station we met Karen Conway, the solicitor Social Services had appointed. She looked very formal in her smart trouser suit and she had a businesslike manner to match.

'Am I going to go to prison?' Meg whispered once we'd sat down.

'Meg, arson is an extremely serious offence,' Karen explained, pulling no punches. 'It's up to a court to decide whether a custodial sentence is appropriate.'

'Just tell the truth and we'll take it from there,' I reassured Meg gently.

I was relieved when I saw that it was PC Hirst who was questioning her. Meg was very tearful and shaky, but I sat with her, holding her hand, while she gave them a statement about what she'd done.

'Meg, I'm charging you with two counts of arson relating to the fire at Mildred House and the fire in the shed at your foster carer Maggie's house,' PC Hirst told her firmly when she'd finished.

'We're going to release you on bail and you'll have to appear at the youth court in three days.'

Meg burst into tears.

'I'm so sorry,' she whimpered, curling up in a ball on the chair. 'I didn't mean it.'

Despite the seriousness of what she'd done, I could see she was absolutely distraught and I wished I could take some of her pain away.

'Maggie will take you home now, Meg,' the solicitor told her kindly.

I helped her up and practically carried her out to the car.

'Well done for telling the truth,' I told her. 'That's the worst bit over and done with.'

Meg didn't say a word. She looked terrified, and I was reminded again of how young she really was.

That night when we got home, I left Meg curled up in her bedroom and Louisa and I helped Isla to pack.

'She's so pleased to be leaving,' Louisa said to me sadly when Isla had gone to sort out her toys downstairs. 'Anyone would think it had been awful here.'

'She's just excited about going home.' I smiled. 'It's no reflection on us.'

Nonetheless, I had to admit that I was still feeling very sad as I folded up Isla's clean clothes and put them neatly into her case.

That night I tucked her in for the last time.

'I've really missed my mummy,' she sighed. 'I can't wait to be back in my bedroom at home.'

'I know you have, flower.' I smiled, ruffling her gorgeous curls. 'And I know your mummy's missed you lots.'

'I've liked being at your house though, Maggie,' she added.

'And we've loved having you,' I told her. 'Now get some sleep because you've got an exciting day ahead of you tomorrow.'

Even when a child was only with me for a short time it was always hard to say goodbye. I knew the house would feel very empty without happy little Isla. I was going to miss her crazy curls and her endless chatter. It would just be me, Louisa and Meg and the start of what was going to be a difficult few weeks. As I sank into bed that night, my stomach was knotted with dread at the thought of what was to come.

SEVEN

Judgement Day

Meg's face was frozen with fear and I could see that she was on the verge of tears as we walked into the court. I grabbed her hand and gave it a squeeze for moral support.

'The district judge will be here soon,' Karen the solicitor explained.

The youth court was held in a special sitting at the local magistrate's court. Members of the public weren't allowed in so I was surprised to see a thin blonde woman sitting in the public gallery.

'Do you know who that is?' I asked Karen, confused.

'That's Zoe, Meg's mother,' she whispered. 'Parents are allowed to sit in on proceedings.'

When Meg saw her, all of her previous anger seemed to dissolve and she went running over to her.

'Mum!' she sobbed. 'I'm so sorry.'

'It's going to be OK, Meg,' cried Zoe, reaching out for her hand.

'Meg, we have to go and sit down,' said Karen, gently ushering her away. 'The judge will be here soon.'

Thankfully in a youth court the child sits in the well of the court rather than having to stand in a dock. Meg sat at the front with Karen while I went and sat with Zoe.

'It's nice to meet you at last,' I said, introducing myself.

'Oh, Maggie, I'm so sorry about everything,' she sighed. 'Your shed, the fire, the children's home. I had no idea Meg would do anything like that.'

'None of us did,' I replied sympathetically. 'It's not your fault.'

However, I could tell that she was shouldering the blame.

There was no more time to chat as the district judge walked into the court. He was a stern-looking man in his sixties who stared over his wire-framed glasses at Meg.

'You're charged with two counts of arson to which you've offered the court a guilty plea,' he told her.

'Yes, sir, that's correct,' Karen confirmed, speaking on Meg's behalf.

'I'll see you again in six weeks for sentencing.' He nodded. 'That should be adequate time for pre-sentencing reports to be carried out.'

'Thank you, sir,' replied Karen.

It was all over in seconds. I wasn't sure what I had been expecting but I felt a bit shell-shocked at how quickly it was all over and done with.

'What does that mean?' asked Meg, looking puzzled as the judge and the clerks left the court. 'Am I going to prison?'

'He's not going to decide for a few weeks and I'm afraid we can't predict what his decision is going to be,' Karen explained.

For the next few weeks we were all going to be living in limbo.

*

As long as I had Meg with me, I wasn't able to foster any other children as it was too much of a risk. The house remained in lockdown so Meg wasn't able to go into any of the rooms downstairs on her own. Every day I'd do a quick search of her bedroom and when she came in from school I'd look through her bag to check she didn't have any lighters or matches on her. I felt like a prison guard rather than a foster carer and I was constantly checking up on Meg, keeping an eye on where she was in the house and what she was doing.

Since her arson had been uncovered she'd shot to the top of the waiting list for therapy and she started seeing a counsellor as well as a child psychologist. Once we knew the outcome of the court case, then Meg and Zoe would hopefully start family therapy too. However, this was all dependent on her not being sent to a young offenders' institution and there were no guarantees. Karen had warned us that arson where there was a risk to life usually carried with it a custodial sentence.

Meg had completely changed from the surly girl I'd been living with before. She was very weepy and her anger had turned to upset and grief. I tried my best to reassure her.

'Would you like to talk to your mum?' I asked Meg one weekend. 'I'm sure she'd love to speak to you.'

'Am I allowed?' she asked meekly.

'Of course you are,' I said. 'You can speak to her whenever you want.'

'I think I'd like that,' she told me.

Zoe was delighted that Meg wanted to talk to her.

'What's going to happen to me, Mum?' she sobbed down the phone. 'If I go to prison, will you come and visit me?'

'Of course I will, sweetheart,' Zoe told her. 'But hopefully it won't come to that.'

Before she hung up, I had a quick chat to Zoe.

'Why don't you come round and see her here?' I suggested. 'I think Meg would really like that.'

'Are you sure?' asked Zoe, surprised. 'It's caused so many arguments in the past.'

'I think things are different now,' I explained. 'Meg's realised what she has to lose. She needs your reassurance.'

I decided it was best not to tell Meg about Zoe's visit in case it made her anxious. Zoe's visit a few days later was timed for her to be already there when Meg got home from school. I could see she was nervous about how Meg was going to react when she saw her.

'If there's any problem, we can cut the visit short and you can go,' I reassured her.

But when Meg came in and saw her mum, she stopped dead in her tracks.

'Hi, Meg,' said Zoe nervously. 'I can't stop thinking about you since I saw you at court. I wanted to come and see you and spend some time with you.'

Meg's face crumpled and she burst into tears.

'Thank you, Mum,' she sobbed. 'I'm so glad you've come. If I go to prison I ain't going to be able to see you and I'd hate that.'

It was strange, but after everything that had happened, the terrible things that Meg had done were bringing the two of them together again and they were talking properly for the first time in months. I went to put the kettle on in the kitchen and when I came back, I peeped through the door of the living room to see how they were getting on.

Zoe and Meg were sitting on the sofa together. Meg was leaning into Zoe as her mum stroked her long dark hair.

'Remember I used to do this when you were little?' Zoe said to her. 'You'd make me do this for hours until you fell asleep.'

Meg nodded and gave her a smile.

'I'm sorry for being so horrible, Mum,' she sighed. 'I don't blame you for hating me.'

'Meg, darling, I've never, ever hated you,' sighed Zoe, looking visibly upset. 'I love you. I always have and I always will. I didn't like how you were behaving or the people you were hanging round with but I felt powerless to do anything about it. I felt I had to put you in care to try and stop you. I was desperate and it was the only way I thought I could keep you safe.'

'I thought you put me in care cos you didn't want me any more,' replied Meg, her voice breaking.

'Oh, sweetie, I'm so sorry,' sighed Zoe. 'Of course I want you. You're my daughter and you always will be. I just couldn't cope. I was at the end of my tether and I didn't know what else to do. I'm so sorry for letting you down.'

Zoe started to cry too and Meg nestled into her shoulder as the pair tried to comfort each other.

I was going to bring them a cup of tea but I was decided it was best not to disturb them. For the first time in months they were talking properly.

I'd seen so many parents and children stuck in these cycles of anger and hurt. Sometimes, sadly, it took a tragedy or a huge upset to shock them out of it. Meg was genuinely frightened about what was going to happen to her and she wanted her mum.

'Will you come and see me again?' Meg asked Zoe when it was time to leave.

Zoe glanced at me for approval before looking back at her daughter.

'If you want me to, then of course I will.' She smiled.

I walked Zoe to the front door and I could see that she was close to tears again.

'She's like a different girl,' she told me, astonished. 'That's the first time she's let me cuddle her in years.'

'She's finally getting the help she needs and she's realising what she has to lose,' I told her, smiling sadly.

Seven long weeks after Meg had been charged, we went back to court for her to be sentenced. It was a day that we all knew had to come but one that we'd been dreading. I knew it had been preying on Meg's mind as well as mine. Neither of us had been sleeping properly and I'd often find her lying in bed wide awake late at night. The hard thing was, I couldn't even reassure her that everything was going to be OK because I didn't know that it was. Neither of us knew what the judge was going to decide and it was so hard for her having her future in someone else's hands.

Zoe and I sat in the public gallery together. I could feel her body trembling and she picked nervously at the tissue clutched in her hands.

'I don't know what I'll do if she goes to prison,' she mumbled. 'How will she cope? Things are just starting to get better with us.'

'It's going to be OK,' I soothed, praying that I was right.

I wasn't so sure when I saw the district judge's serious face.

'Well, Meg,' he said, looking over his glasses at her. 'As I'm sure you know, arson is an extremely serious offence. You were very lucky that the fire in the children's home didn't result in loss of life otherwise you'd be appearing in front of this court on very different charges.'

Next to me, Zoe burst into tears and I gave her arm a reassuring pat. I held my breath as the judge looked through the papers.

'There *are* mitigating circumstances,' he said. 'I know you were distressed after recently been put into the care system and having to leave your family home.'

Zoe let out a little sob next to me.

'The report from your psychologist says you were suffering from anger issues and lighting fires was an outlet for that. I also know from your social worker that since you confessed, you haven't been involved in any more incidents.'

He paused. I could see Meg's head shaking with fear.

'Therefore, taking everything into account . . .' he continued. I held my breath.

'. . . I'm going to give you a conditional discharge on the premise that you don't ever set fire to anything again. This will be for the next six years until you reach the age of eighteen. If you do, you will be back in front of the courts and the next judge will not be so lenient. Do you understand?' he asked her sternly.

'Yes,' whimpered Meg.

My body sank in relief.

Thank goodness.

'What's a discharge?' gasped Zoe. 'What does that mean?'

'It means that she's not going to a young offenders' institution,' I told her. 'It's good news. She's free.'

Zoe burst into tears again but this time they were tears of relief. As Meg walked towards us, Zoe ran down to give her a hug.

'How do you feel?' I asked Meg.

'Sick,' she sighed, her face pale and tear-streaked.

'You were very, very lucky,' Karen told her.

As we left the court there was no celebration or sense of jubilation. We were all just utterly relieved.

The following day Angela came round to see us.

'I've got some good news,' she told Meg. 'I've just had a call from Mildred House. The renovation work has finished on your wing so you should be able to move back by the end of this week.'

'Move?' she frowned. 'But why can't I stay here with Maggie?'

'Maggie's house was always a short-term solution,' Angela told her. 'You're very lucky that the children's home is willing to have you back after what happened with the fire.'

'But I don't wanna go back,' wailed Meg.

'Meg, Angela's right,' I told her. 'Your friends are there and your schooling. You won't have to go back and forth any more.'

'You're a liar,' she spat. 'You don't care just like my mum. You said you'd be there for me and now you can't wait to get rid of me.'

'That's not true,' I told her. 'I do care and I'll always be there for you. I'll come and visit you and you can come and see us.'

It was hard for her to accept but I knew in my heart that the children's home was the right place for Meg. In all honesty it had been exhausting trying to keep an eye on her 24/7. I hadn't been sleeping well as I was still terrified of the thought of being woken by a fire. At Mildred House there were staff always on duty and I also knew CCTV had now been fitted into the building in all of the communal areas.

Also, having Meg in the house meant I hadn't been able to foster any other children. Fostering was not only my vocation but also my livelihood and I needed to keep fostering to pay my mortgage.

'Well, it ain't fair,' yelled Meg, storming upstairs to her room.

'I'm sure in time she'll get used to the idea,' said Angela. 'I'm happy to take her to Mildred House on Friday.'

'What do you think about Zoe going with her instead?' I suggested. 'They've been getting on much better lately and that might help soften the blow.'

'That's a great idea if she'd be willing,' replied Angela.

Thankfully, Zoe was more than happy to be involved. Over the next couple of days I helped Meg pack up her things. She didn't have much as a lot of it had been damaged in the fire. As a goodbye gift I bought her a new duvet cover with clouds on it and a matching lamp.

'These are for your room at Mildred House,' I told her. 'A little bird told me the walls in your bedroom have been repainted blue so I thought they would go nicely.'

'Thank you.' She smiled, looking pleased.

Louisa had bought her a set of pens and pencils as she'd started drawing a lot recently.

Meg looked astonished, and I could tell that she was delighted with the present.

'Take care, Meg,' Louisa told her, giving her a hug that morning before she went to work.

'Bye, Louisa.' Meg smiled shyly. I couldn't believe how different she was from the angry girl that had arrived at my house all those weeks before.

'Right, I think you're all set.' I smiled. 'Your mum should be here in a minute.'

When Zoe arrived I helped her pack up the car. There was no more putting it off – the time had come to say goodbye. Meg hung around in the hallway and I could see her brown eyes were brimming with tears. The last thing I wanted was a big emotional scene and for her to get upset so I knew I had to keep my own emotions in check.

'Bye, lovey,' I said to Meg, giving her a hug. 'You take care and behave yourself.'

'Don't worry, I'm not gonna light any more fires,' she said, giving me a weak smile. 'Thanks for not hating me.'

'I don't hate you,' I promised her. 'I only ever wanted to help you.'

As she walked out to the car, I said my goodbyes to Zoe.

'Thanks for everything, Maggie,' she told me. 'Thanks for being a mother to my daughter when I couldn't be. Thank you for going through all this turmoil with her.'

'It's been my pleasure,' I said. 'And don't worry, I'm sure Meg will be OK at Mildred House.'

'Actually things are going really well between us so I'm hoping she won't need to be there long.' Zoe smiled. 'We're starting family therapy in a couple of weeks so we'll see how that goes.'

'I really hope it works out for you all,' I said.

I watched them get into the car and swallowed the lump in my throat. As she drove off down the road with her mum, I was full of hope for Meg. Hope that she had finally put the past behind her and was able to move on. And hope that one day, she would return home and be part of her family again.

Not to Blame

ONE

Tea and Sympathy

The clatter of teacups and the hum of chatter echoed down the corridor.

'It sounds like it's going to be a busy one today,' my friend and fellow foster carer Vicky said.

We'd popped in to a support group run by the fostering agency that we both worked for. Once a month, they organised a coffee morning where you could drop in and chat to other foster carers and get another person's opinion or advice, share your concerns or even have a sympathetic shoulder to cry on when you needed it. It wasn't just about problems either. It was always very sociable and I liked going as it was a chance to catch up with other carers that perhaps I hadn't seen for a while.

I was happy to help others too if it was needed. As someone who had been fostering for years, my agency often put me in touch with other less experienced carers of theirs who were going through a difficult time and needed someone to talk to.

These sessions were always well attended and today, as we pushed open the door, I could see the room was packed. I went over to the kettle to make Vicky and myself a cup of tea while she went to find us a couple of spare seats.

'How are you, Maggie?' asked a woman called Pat who I recognised from agency events. 'Are your placements going well?'

'Good, thank you.' I smiled. 'Yes, really well actually. I've got two lovely boys with me at the moment.'

I was currently fostering Albie and Ethan, seven-year-old identical twins, who had come to me a month ago. Their mother Liz had recently had a breakdown and was in hospital. Their father Martin had tried to care for them, but he had also suffered with depression in the past and had struggled to cope with the boys' needs without support. Although the boys had been scared to be taken into care at first, they had quickly settled in to living with me. They still had contact with their parents three times a week and the hope was that they would eventually be able to go back home.

By the time I'd made the tea and taken it over to where Vicky was sitting, I could see she was deep in conversation with another foster carer who I didn't recognise. I went and sat down quietly next to them, as I could see the woman was upset and I didn't want to interrupt her. As she spoke, it was clear her current placement was the reason for her upset.

'Oh, it's been meltdown after meltdown and it's just so exhausting,' she sighed. 'It's like living with a toddler, not a sixteen-year-old. She's so scatty, things are constantly getting lost and broken and as for her personal hygiene . . .' She wrinkled up her nose.

'Anyway, I've had it. She's worn me down so I've given notice. I feel guilty as I know I'm not the first foster carer to do that to her, but I just can't cope with her any longer. I've tried and tried to help her, but ultimately it's not worth jeopardising my marriage or my mental health any more.'

I felt sorry for her as I listened to her talk. The reality is that being a foster carer can sometimes be very isolating, particularly when you have a child living with you who is particularly challenging. There's no respite when someone is living in your home with you 24/7: there is no way of getting away from it. Supervising social workers and our fostering agency were always very supportive, but unless a person is actually living the experience with you, it can be very difficult for people to understand. That's why these support groups were such a lifeline. Foster carers could come along and be honest about how they were feeling and get support from other carers without any fear of judgement.

The woman got up to make a coffee, giving us both a weak smile as she left, and I handed Vicky her tea.

'She sounded upset,' I sighed.

She nodded. 'She's been having a hard time with her current placement – a sixteen-year-old girl. It sounds like she's been round quite a few carers in the county before her too.

'I'm surprised she hasn't been to your house yet, Maggie,' she joked.

Vicky always teased me about the fact that I liked difficult teenagers. I found them really interesting and most of the time they didn't phase me. Often, when a particularly challenging older child came into the care system, I was asked to take them on if I was free.

'I can't help it if I'm the teen whisperer,' I laughed.

In the end, I had a lovely couple of hours at the coffee morning. I had a good catch-up with Vicky and chatted to some other carers. Afterwards I headed home to get lunch and to do some tidying before it was time to pick the twins up from school.

I was halfway through a cheese sandwich when my mobile rang. It was my supervising social worker, Becky. She hadn't been in the office earlier when I'd popped in before the coffee morning, so I assumed that one of her colleagues had told her I'd been looking for her and she was just calling to say hello.

I was wrong.

'Maggie, I wanted to chat to you about a possible placement,' she told me. 'How would you feel about taking on a teenager?'

'Oh,' I gasped, quickly swallowing my mouthful of sandwich. 'You've caught me a bit off guard there.'

I listened as she told me more. She had just had a call from Social Services about a sixteen-year-old girl.

'All I know is that she's been in and out of the care system since birth,' she told me. 'She's actually coming from another foster carer in the area who has just given notice on her as she's struggling to cope with her difficult behaviour.'

My thoughts immediately went back to the support group earlier that morning and the foster carer who had been talking to Vicky. Hadn't she just given notice on a girl exactly the same age? I knew Becky would always try not to name names and tell me which carer she was moving on from, but surely it was too much of a coincidence for it not to be the same girl?

'I know you have an affinity with tricky teenagers, Maggie, so I thought I'd try you first,' Becky said. 'Do you want to have a think about it and call me back?'

It was an easy decision for me. Albie and Ethan were pretty settled and I hadn't had any problems with them. I could cope with one more.

'I don't need to think about it,' I told Becky. 'I'd be happy to help.'

As was often the case with children who needed somewhere to live at short notice, Becky didn't have many other details about the girl or how long she was likely to be with me.

'All I know is that she's got the same name as me,' she told me. 'But she's a Rebecca rather than a Becky. I'll ask Trish, the social worker, to come round to see you in the morning after you're back from dropping the boys at school – she should be able to give you a bit more information about her.'

'Thanks,' I said. 'I'm looking forward to finding out more.'

As I put the phone down, I experienced the strange mix of adrenalin, nerves and excitement that I always felt when I knew a new placement was on its way. I wolfed down my sandwich and then spent the rest of the afternoon sorting out the bedrooms. Albie and Ethan were in the bigger bedroom in bunk beds and I had another spare single room where Rebecca could sleep. I made sure there were clean sheets on the bed and removed a few toys that were still in there from a previous placement. I put a couple of cushions on the bed and a pretty rug on the floor to make it look a bit more girly and grown-up.

That afternoon when I picked the boys up from school, I decided it would be best not to mention Rebecca coming to stay with us. I'd learnt from my many years fostering that things could quickly change in the care system. Sometimes there could be a sudden change of plan and children who were meant to be coming to me for whatever reason didn't. Kids the twins' age tended to live in the moment and I didn't want to tell them someone else was coming to live with us and then it not happen. I decided that I would wait until I'd spoken to Rebecca's social worker and everything had been confirmed. The boys had been little troupers and they had both been so stoic about being separated from their parents, but I could see the sadness in their eyes during contact every time they asked their dad how Mummy was. They both understood that she wasn't very well and needed to have a rest in hospital for a little while, but it was clear that they missed her enormously. The boys may have looked identical with their big brown eyes and floppy brown hair, but their personalities were quite different. Albie was very happy-go-lucky while Ethan was a bit quieter and more serious, but they were both football-mad and I'd got used to kickabouts in the park and endless discussions about their favourite team, Manchester United.

That night I tossed and turned, my mind filled with thoughts about Rebecca and what she was going to be like. I was still convinced that it was the same girl the foster carer had been talking about at the support group this morning. Her words ran through my head – constant meltdowns, hygiene problems, how she had worn her down.

She had seemed like a competent carer, so why should my experience be any different? Would I be able to cope with this girl if so many other carers hadn't been able to? Common sense told me to wait until I'd spoken to her social worker, but in my head I couldn't help but prepare myself for the worst. Part of me was also intrigued. At sixteen, Rebecca was old to still be living with a foster carer. By that age, children had normally been found a place in a children's home or were moved into semi-independent living where they lived in their own room or flat with an adult supervising them.

The following morning, tired from a restless night's sleep, my stomach was still knotted with nerves as I drove home after dropping the boys at school. I made myself a coffee and then sat on the sofa anxiously waiting for the social worker's knock on the door.

When my phone rang, I jumped in shock, startled from my reverie, but to my surprise, it was Louisa. Louisa had come to live with me when she was thirteen after her parents had been tragically killed in a car crash. She'd lived with me right up until a couple of years ago when she'd got married and I couldn't have been closer to her if she had been my own daughter. She was twenty-four now, and worked as a nanny. She and her husband Charlie had a flat just ten minutes away from my house. I spoke to her every couple of days and she often popped in for her tea.

'I'm afraid I can't talk at the minute, lovey,' I told her. 'I've got a social worker arriving any minute to talk to me about a new placement.'

'No problem,' she replied. 'I just had the morning off so I thought I'd ring for a chat. Call me when you get chance.'

In all the years she had lived with me, Louisa had grown accustomed to new foster children arriving and leaving, so she was more than familiar with what fostering entailed, and I knew she wouldn't take offence at me needing to get her off the phone.

As soon as I hung up, I heard a rap on the front door. I opened it to find a woman who looked like she was in her early fifties, and was petite with very short grey hair and striking bright blue glasses on a gold chain.

'You must be Trish.' I smiled. 'Come on in.'

I made her a coffee and we sat at the kitchen table.

'So let me tell you a bit more about Rebecca,' she began, once we were settled.

I listened as she told me how Rebecca had been in the care system all her life, after her teenage mother had given her up for adoption at birth.

'It was a different local authority in another part of the country and as she was placed into care voluntarily, there isn't much information on her file,' she added. 'Just that her mum had very little medical care during her pregnancy, she lived in hostels and had no family support. She was born prematurely but medically seemed OK.'

She described how Rebecca had been adopted as a newborn. When she was eight, her adoptive parents had divorced. She had always been a challenging child and now she was on her own, her adoptive mum simply couldn't cope.

'It's been the same story ever since,' said Trish. 'Massive meltdowns, angry outbursts, smashing things up. By the time she was twelve, she was back in the care system and has been in and out of various children's homes and foster carers ever since.'

'Does she still have contact with her adopted mum?' I asked.

'Sadly, it appears not,' replied Trish. 'Neither of them wanted it apparently and Rebecca was moved to a children's home out of the county. She's been moved wherever there's a space, so over the years she's been up and down the country and passed around different authorities,' she sighed.

We both knew the system. Sadly there were more children than there were places to take them, so it was often a lottery as to where they ended up.

I felt so sad hearing about this young woman's life. It seemed as though she'd had so little stability, and it was no wonder this had taken its toll on her emotionally.

'I'm curious as to why, at her age, you're looking to place her with a foster carer?' I asked.

'It's because she's emotionally disadvantaged,' sighed Trish.

I wasn't one for buzzwords and jargon. 'What does that actually mean?' I asked her, confused.

'Well, she doesn't act like an average sixteen-year-old,' she told me. 'She's emotionally very immature. She has difficulty making friends and in the past people have taken advantage of her, so she's much safer in a home environment. She's very disorganised and struggles with everyday tasks.'

I asked about her education and if she was still in school.

'As far as I can see from her records, she's always struggled at school,' replied Trish. 'She finds it difficult to retain information. She wasn't entered for GCSEs and instead has done entry-level maths and English that were lower-level qualifications.

'A couple of months ago we managed to get her an apprenticeship at a hairdresser's, but I think they're starting to lose patience with her, to be honest. Half the time she doesn't turn up, and when she does, she's often late.'

I asked about special needs but Trish shrugged.

'She's been to so many schools over the years in so many different places, I don't think she's ever been properly assessed,' she told me. 'I think it probably all just boils down to attachment issues, though.'

It was so sad to hear of a young person being able to fall through the cracks like that.

'If you can take her for now, Maggie, then all the relevant people can get their heads together and work out the long-term plan for her. Despite everything I've told you, she's a lovely girl,' Trish added, as if she was suddenly worried that I might be having second thoughts about taking her. 'She's just a bit scatty and she has these outbursts.'

There was one question that had been preying on my mind while Trish had been talking.

'Has she ever been physically violent towards any of her carers?' I asked.

To my relief, Trish shook her head.

'Rebecca does have tantrums and occasionally she's been known to smash things but she's never hurt anyone.'

I had to bear the twins in mind in all this. I didn't want them to ever witness another foster child physically attacking me, and violence would have been a deal-breaker for me, having younger children in the house.

With that settled, all that was left was for me to meet Rebecca.

'How would you feel if I brought her round to you later on this afternoon?' Trish asked. 'She's not gone to work today so I could go round to her foster carer's now and help her pack her things, then bring her back here?'

'Yes, that's fine,' I told her. 'Her room's all ready for her. It would be great if you could bring her round later on this afternoon after I've done the school run. That way it would give me a chance to tell the boys on the drive home.'

'OK, great, thanks, Maggie,' said Trisha, getting up to leave. 'I'll see you later.'

When Trish had left, I sat back down at the kitchen table to gather my thoughts before I called Louisa back. I was curious to meet Rebecca. Whatever her behaviour was like, the poor girl had spent the majority of her life being passed from pillar to post. She needed continuity, stability, love and care. I just hoped that I was able to give it to her and, above all, that I would be able to cope with what lay ahead.

TWO

An Open Door

Two identical little faces stared back at me as I talked them through what was happening.

'So, Rebecca is going to come round this afternoon with her social worker and then she's going to live here too for a little while,' I gently explained to Albie and Ethan.

'Is the big girl going to sleep in our room?' Albie asked, his huge brown eyes filled with confusion.

'That's a really good question, sweetie.' I smiled. 'You do have another bed in your room but because Rebecca's a teenager, she's going to have her own bedroom with her own bed. Does that sound OK?'

Both boys nodded.

'Is there anything else you want to ask?'

'Does she like Lego?' asked Ethan.

'I don't know the answer to that,' I told him. 'But when she gets here later you can ask her yourself.'

The twins had seemed puzzled at first when I'd told them that another child was coming to live at my house with them.

But now I'd answered their questions, they seemed intrigued about meeting her. I know I certainly was.

'Will she eat tea with us?' Ethan asked.

'I hope so, lovey,' I replied. 'I've made a shepherd's pie big enough for four so hopefully she'll be here very soon.'

It was just before 5 p.m. when the knock at the door came. As soon as the twins heard it, they jumped up and ran out into the hallway. Then they hesitated and stood back nervously while I opened the door.

Trish stood there carrying a small suitcase and next to her was a girl I assumed to be Rebecca. Her long dark hair was tangled and greasy like it hadn't been washed in a while and she had a small, sweet face with dainty features.

'Hello again, Maggie,' said Trish. 'This is Rebecca.'

'Lovely to meet you, Rebecca.' I grinned. 'Come on in.'

She gave me a weak smile in return. She looked scruffy and unkempt in a baggy, holey sweatshirt and a pair of leggings that looked way too small for her. She was carrying a rucksack that was stuffed to the brim. The top was hanging open and it looked as though everything might fall out at any minute.

'This is Ethan and Albie who are also living with me for a little while,' I told her, gesturing to the boys, who were staring up at her in awe.

The boys smiled shyly but Rebecca was preoccupied with rummaging through her bag and didn't seem to be paying any attention to what I was saying.

'Where's my phone?' she asked Trish frantically. 'Have you seen my phone?'

'You had it earlier when you got in the car,' Trish told her. 'We'll have a look in a minute.'

'No, I need to find it now,' she snapped. 'What if I've dropped it? It might be in your car, or maybe it fell out on the road?'

'Sorry, Maggie,' said Trish apologetically.

'Don't worry,' I told her. 'Why don't you two try and find the phone and I'll go and settle the boys down in front of the TV.'

By the time I'd put a DVD on for the boys, Rebecca and Trish were in the kitchen. Rebecca had thankfully found her mobile.

'Where was it?' I asked.

'In her bag exactly where she had put it,' sighed Trish wearily.

I could see her patience with Rebecca was already wearing thin.

'Would anyone like a drink?' I asked cheerily, quickly changing the subject.

'I'd love a cup of tea please,' replied Trish.

Rebecca shook her head.

'How long am I here for?' she asked Trish. 'Am I just staying for one night?'

'Remember we discussed this earlier,' Trish told her patiently. 'You're going to be staying with Maggie for a while until we work out a long-term plan for you.'

'I don't see why I've got to come to another foster place,' she sighed. 'Why can't I get my own flat?'

'We already talked about that, Rebecca, and we said that we don't feel that you're ready for that yet and anyway it can't happen until you're at least seventeen.'

'But I *am* seventeen in a few weeks,' she sighed.

'Well that's something I'll be talking to my managers about and we will have to wait and see,' said Trish.

Rebecca huffed and puffed and it was clear from her expression that she wasn't happy about the situation.

'Rebecca, why don't I take you upstairs and show you the bedroom where you're going to be sleeping, then you can unpack your stuff and settle in while Trish and I have a chat?' I suggested.

'Suppose so,' she grumbled.

Trish stayed in the kitchen while I carried Rebecca's case upstairs and showed her to the single room.

'There are some drawers there you can put your things in and some hangers in the wardrobe,' I told her.

She shook her head.

'Nah, I'll just leave my stuff in the case,' she sighed. 'No point getting it out. I ain't gonna be here long, am I?'

'I think it would be a good idea to unpack,' I told her gently. 'Like Trish said, what Social Services are going to be doing is working out a plan for what's best for you until you reach eighteen and that might take a bit of time.'

The message didn't seem to be getting through that this might not be as temporary as she thought.

I left Rebecca to it and went down to see Trish in the kitchen.

'She seems OK,' I told her, as I made us both a cup of tea. 'Although she keeps asking how long she's going to be here.'

'Oh, don't worry,' said Trish. 'She always asks the same questions on repeat. She's so forgetful – it's like she doesn't listen to a word you're saying.'

'I find most teenagers are like that.' I smiled. 'They have selective memories when it comes to things they don't want to hear.'

Trish drank her tea and I went through some paperwork with her.

'Is she due at work at the hairdresser's tomorrow?' I asked her.

Trish nodded.

'She starts at 9 a.m. Even though she's been there six months, I still think it's worth you reminding her and making sure that she's up and dressed in the morning. She's not very good at motivating herself.'

Trish explained that my house was closer to the salon where Rebecca worked than her previous placement had been.

'It's only four stops on the bus and I've talked her through the route twice today and shown her as well,' she told me. 'She won't have to leave here until around 8.45 a.m.'

It posed a slight problem in that I had to leave half an hour earlier to drive the twins to their primary school in another town.

'Are you OK about me leaving her in the house in the morning on her own while I do the school run?' I asked Trish.

'Of course,' she replied. 'You have to take the boys to school.'

It wasn't ideal for me as generally I didn't like to leave foster children alone in the house, even if they were older teenagers, and especially not someone who had just arrived. I didn't know Rebecca and I didn't know whether or not I could trust her yet on her own, but if she had to be at work at nine o'clock, it seemed that there wasn't really any other way around it.

Trish gulped down the last of her tea and I could see that she was keen to leave.

'I'm going to head back now, Maggie,' she said. 'I have to call in at the office to do some paperwork and it's been a long day. I'll just nip up and say goodbye to Rebecca.'

When she came back down, I walked her to the front door.

'I hope she has a settled first night,' she said. 'Any problems, then give me a ring.'

'I'm sure we'll be fine,' I told her.

After she'd gone, I went upstairs to check on Rebecca. She was sitting on the bed flicking through her phone.

'Oh, you've not unpacked yet,' I said, noticing that her case and bag were still on the floor where I'd left them.

'Oh, sorry,' she said, looking surprised to see the bags still on the floor. 'I forgot.'

'Don't worry,' I told her. 'I'm just about to do dinner so come down to the kitchen whenever you're sorted.'

'OK,' she said. 'How long am I staying here? Is it just one night?'

I knew the poor girl was probably just trying to get things straight in her head, which is why she kept asking the same question over and over again.

'Remember what we said earlier? Trish is going to be talking to her managers about what's best for you long term but that might take a little while. So until then, you're going to be here with me.'

'Why can't I get my own flat?' she asked.

'Like Trish said before, that can't happen until you're at least seventeen,' I said.

'Oh, OK.' She nodded, looking placated.

Although Trish had described her as ditzy, all I could think about was how many times she'd been moved, how many homes like mine she'd arrived in and left. It was no wonder that the poor girl was so confused.

Rebecca came down just as I was dishing up the dinner.

'What's that?' she asked.

'It's shepherd's pie, lovey.' I smiled, handing her a plate.

'Oh, I don't think I like that,' she replied, scrunching up her nose.

To my relief, though, as soon as the boys came and sat down and started tucking in, she did too. The boys appeared to have got over their shyness, and as we ate, they asked her question after question. Most teenagers would have found that annoying but to give her credit, Rebecca answered them all and was very patient with them.

'Do you like Lego?' Ethan asked her.

'I'm a bit big for Lego,' she told him kindly.

'What toys do you like then?' questioned Albie.

'I don't really have any toys any more cos I'm too old,' she said.

As I cleared the dishes away and watched her chat to them, I couldn't work it out. This was a very different girl to the one Trish had initially described, or the out-of-control teenager I'd heard the woman talking about at the coffee morning. From what I'd seen so far, Rebecca actually seemed quite sweet.

After dinner, I left Rebecca to watch TV while I took the twins upstairs for a bath and stories before bed. After the excitement of Rebecca's arrival, they were particularly hard to settle, and it was after nine o'clock before I came back downstairs.

Rebecca was sitting on the sofa with her mobile, staring blankly at the screen.

'You've had a long day today, so I bet you must be tired,' I said.

'Not really,' she replied.

'Well I think it would probably be a good idea to get ready for bed in the next hour or so as you've got work in the morning,' I told her.

I explained how I tended to lock everything up downstairs by 10.30 p.m. and that I'd like her to have her light out by eleven.

'You might already have seen it but there's a little telly in your room and a CD player if you'd prefer to listen to music.'

It was something I did for older teenagers because it was good for them to have their own space to hang out in when they wanted to, especially if I had younger children living with me and they didn't want to watch kids' TV.

'Do I *have* to go to work tomorrow?' she sighed.

'I'm afraid so,' I told her. 'Trish said the salon was expecting you in.'

Rebecca said she was going to go up to her room to watch TV.

'Please can I have a glass of milk to take with me?' she asked sheepishly.

'Of course you can,' I replied, surprised.

She followed me into the kitchen and watched me open the fridge. But her face dropped when she saw me getting the carton of milk out.

'Oh no, I hate that blue milk,' she snapped. 'I'm not gonna drink that. Have you got any green milk?'

I shook my head.

'I'm afraid I haven't,' I told her. 'The boys prefer full fat so that's all I've got in at the moment. I can nip to the shops tomorrow and get you some semi-skimmed, though, now that I know that you prefer it.'

Rebecca shook her head.

'No, no, I said I'm not gonna drink that blue milk so I need some green milk tonight.'

I couldn't believe how wound up she was getting over something as simple as milk.

'Look, Rebecca, I'm sorry I don't have the milk you like, but it's late, the boys are in bed and you're going to be heading to bed soon too,' I told her firmly. 'No one is going out now to get milk so you'll have to wait until tomorrow. Do you want a glass of water instead?'

'I don't want water,' she hissed angrily. 'I want milk.'

Much to my horror, she swiped her hand across the work surface and knocked the carton of milk onto the floor. I'd already twisted the top loose so a litre of milk pumped out all over the lino.

'Now look what you've done,' she yelled. 'You did that. That's your fault, that is!'

With that, she stormed off upstairs. I looked at the puddle of milk on the floor and sighed. It was such a minor, silly thing to have a meltdown over, but suddenly what Trish had described as a toddler tantrum all became clear.

I wanted to give Rebecca some time to calm down so I mopped up the mess then tidied up downstairs. By this time I was absolutely shattered, so I locked up and headed upstairs.

Before I went to bed, I gently knocked on Rebecca's door. 'Can I come in?' I asked.

There was no answer so I pushed it open. The telly was on and Rebecca was laid on the bed fast asleep on top of the duvet. She was still in her jumper and leggings but she looked in such a deep sleep, I didn't want to wake her. Quietly I turned off the TV and got a blanket out of the wardrobe and gently put it over her.

She was very petite for her age and curled up like that, she looked so vulnerable and much younger than her sixteen years. As I crept out of the room, I couldn't help but notice that her case on the floor was still not unpacked.

The next morning, I was up at 6.30 a.m. as usual so I could get showered and dressed before the twins woke up. By 7.30 a.m. there was still no sign of Rebecca, so I knocked on her door.

'It's time to get up now, Rebecca,' I called. 'I'm finished in the bathroom if you want to have a shower.'

'OK,' groaned a voice.

I went downstairs and got on with making breakfast for the boys and tea for me. But when twenty minutes had passed and there was still no sign of Rebecca, I went upstairs and knocked on her door again.

'Are you awake, Rebecca?' I called. 'You need to get up and have some breakfast now if you're going to get to work on time.'

No answer.

I knocked again.

Silence.

Feeling concerned, I pushed open the door to find Rebecca lying in bed still fast asleep.

'Come on, lovey, you've got to get up now or you'll be late for work,' I told her.

'Oh yes,' she mumbled groggily.

But I had to call her again twice before she finally emerged looking bleary-eyed.

'You'd better hurry up,' I told her. 'You need to get yourself organised for work. It's nearly eight o'clock.'

'Why didn't you wake me?' she snapped.

'I tried several times,' I told her. 'Anyway, you're up now, so get yourself in the shower.'

'I don't want one,' she said. 'I won't bother today.'

Her hair looked lank and greasy but I didn't want to push it when she had just arrived.

'OK, well let's go down and I'll get you some breakfast,' I replied.

As we walked into the kitchen, I realised my error. I'd put a selection of cereals on the kitchen table as well as a fresh carton of full-fat milk – the same type Rebecca had kicked off about the previous night.

Please don't let her have another tantrum, I thought to myself as she sat down at the table. I couldn't cope with it this morning when I was trying to get everybody up and out of the door, and I didn't want the boys to have to witness it. As Rebecca sat down, my heart was in my mouth and I could hardly bear to look. The boys were chattering away to each other and happily tucking into their Weetabix.

'I can do you some toast if you'd prefer?' I suggested tentatively.

'No, cereal's fine.' She smiled, helping herself.

I couldn't believe my eyes as I watched her pour the full-fat milk over some Weetabix. What had all that fuss been about last night? She obviously didn't mind the milk too much if she was putting it all over her cereal.

I made myself a cup of tea and sat down with her.

'So you know where you're going to get to work?' I asked her.

'Yes,' she sighed, rolling her eyes. 'Trish showed me loads of times. Can I have a door key?'

'You won't need one, lovey,' I told her. 'Just shut the door on your way out this morning and then I'll be here tonight when you get back from work.'

'OK,' she said, looking strangely disappointed.

I glanced up at the clock and realised in a panic that it was time for me to take the boys. Even though I did everything in my power to get organised the night before, it was always a rush trying to get the twins out of the door.

'Right, shoes on,' I told them, putting their lunch boxes and water bottles in their bags.

'And have you brushed your teeth?'

'Yes,' they both sighed wearily.

'Have a good day, lovey,' I said to Rebecca. 'Any problems then give me a ring and remember you have to leave by 8.45 like Trish said.'

'OK,' she replied, looking bored.

As I got into the car, I still felt slightly uneasy about leaving her in the house on her own. In fact, I wasn't even convinced that she was actually going to go to work. As I pulled into my street at around half past nine, I was half expecting to find Rebecca still there.

As I walked up the front path, I stopped and did a double take. My front door was wide open.

I ran up the path and into the hallway.

'Rebecca?' I yelled. 'Rebecca? Are you here?'

There was no answer.

Had someone broken in? If the front door was open, I needed to check every room to make sure that no one was in the house.

I frantically ran from room to room. There was no sign of Rebecca anywhere or thankfully anyone else, and nothing seemed to be missing.

As I came down the stairs, I heard a phone ringing, and realised it was Rebecca's mobile, lying on the table in the hallway.

I answered it to a woman called Julie who told me she was calling from the salon where Rebecca worked.

'I'm just calling to see if she's coming in today?' she asked.

Panic rose in my throat.

'Is she not there yet?' I asked.

'No, love. We haven't seen her at all this morning. She was due in half an hour ago.'

Panic rose in my throat. The front door had been wide open, there was no sign of Rebecca and she hadn't got her phone.

Where was she and what on earth had happened?

THREE

Stupid

'Can you do me a favour?' I asked the woman on the phone from the salon. 'If and when Rebecca comes into work, please can you get her to ring me and let me know she's safe?'

I gave her my mobile number and explained that I was Rebecca's foster carer and that she'd just moved to my house.

'Of course,' she said. 'No problem. To be honest, she's never on time so it's more than likely that she's on her way.'

I hoped she was right, but as I put the phone down, I couldn't help but feel a sense of unease. I gave Trish a call and explained what had happened.

'The woman at the salon's right,' she told me. 'She's often late and there have been times when she hasn't turned up at all.'

She paused.

'But I agree it is worrying that the front door was open and she hasn't got her phone with her.'

'She could be anywhere. How long should I give it before I call the police?' I asked her.

'Let's take a view if she's not turned up by lunchtime,' she told me. 'Keep in touch, Maggie.'

I had been due to pop round to Vicky's for a coffee but I couldn't risk leaving the house in case Rebecca came back. I rang Vicky and explained what was going on.

'Gosh, I'm sorry, Maggie,' she sighed. 'That's strange. I hope she turns up soon.'

'So do I,' I replied. 'Her work is only ten minutes away so she should have been there ages ago.'

She'd barely been with me twelve hours and she'd already gone missing. I decided to tackle some paperwork to try and take my mind off things but my stomach churned with worry as I constantly checked the time. Just before half past eleven, I was about to call Trish back when my mobile rang. It was a number I didn't recognise.

'Maggie, it's me,' said a quiet voice.

'Rebecca!' I gasped. 'Where are you?'

'Er, at work,' she replied as if I was asking a ridiculous question.

'What took you so long?' I asked. 'I've been so worried about you.'

'I'm fine,' she added. 'I just got a bit lost on the way to the salon. I'm no good with directions.'

Two and a half hours late sounded more than a bit lost to me!

'Rebecca, you left your phone here so no one could get hold of you,' I told her, exasperated. 'We didn't know what had happened to you.'

'It's not my fault,' she snapped. 'I just didn't pick it up.'

'The front door was wide open too when I got home,' I added. 'Anyone could have walked in. It's lucky nothing was stolen.'

190

'Was it?' she said vaguely. 'I must have forgot to shut it.'

I didn't want to give her too hard a time and upset her at work.

'I'm just glad that you're OK,' I told her gently. 'Do you think you can find your way back here tonight?'

'Yes,' she sighed wearily. 'I'm not stupid, you know.'

'Well if you change your mind, give me a ring and I'll come and pick you up,' I replied.

I felt exasperated as I put the phone down but I knew I couldn't be that cross with her. She'd only been at my house for a night and I knew it must be really unsettling having to cope with yet another move.

I rang Trish to update her.

'What a relief,' she sighed. 'I was literally about to put in a call to the police.'

'After what happened today, I don't think I can risk leaving her alone in the house in the mornings,' I told her. 'If it's OK with you, I'll drop her off at the salon before I take the boys. I know she'll be at work early but I can't see any other solution.'

'Of course, Maggie, I completely understand,' replied Trisha. 'As long as you're sure you can manage that.'

'I think it will be a lot easier than worrying if the house has been locked up and if she's made it to work safely,' I told her.

Trish told me that there was a café a few doors down from the salon.

'I'm sure she could go in there and have a drink until the salon opens,' she told me.

Now I knew Rebecca was OK, I should have been relieved but instead the rest of the day was spent on tenterhooks, worrying that she might go missing again that evening. I couldn't take my eyes off the clock after I'd picked the boys up from school, so I was thankful when I heard her rap on the door just after five.

When she came in, Rebecca wouldn't make eye contact with me.

'I'm sorry about the front door,' she said sheepishly, staring at the floor. 'I didn't notice. Sometimes I do silly things.'

'It's OK,' I told her gently. 'None of us are perfect.'

She followed me into the kitchen and I got her a glass of juice and a biscuit.

'Trish and I were talking and we think it's a good idea for me to take you to work in the mornings,' I told her. 'If we all leave at eight o'clock then I can drop you off at the salon before I take the twins.'

'But that's not fair,' she cried. 'That's way too early.'

'Trish said there's a café near the salon so you could go in there and have a cup of tea before work.'

I could see she wasn't happy about it but after what had happened today, it felt like the only solution.

So from then on, that's what we did. It was stressful getting everyone up and out of the door by eight. Rebecca needed more reminders than the twins and I literally had to drag her out of bed each morning, nag her to brush her teeth and eat her breakfast.

By the third day, I realised I hadn't noticed her have a bath or shower and the towel I'd given her was still folded up in her room where I'd left it when she'd first arrived.

'Rebecca, you need to have a wash,' I told her that evening.

'I'm fine,' she told me. 'I had a shower the other day.'

'I'm pretty sure that you didn't,' I replied.

I didn't want to be cruel but she needed to know the truth.

'I'm sorry, sweetie, but you're starting to smell and it's not very professional to turn up to work at a hairdresser's with dirty hair.'

'Do I have to?' she sighed.

'Yes, you do,' I told her. 'You need to be responsible for keeping yourself clean.'

It was worse than dealing with a toddler. Reluctantly, she stomped upstairs to run a bath while I played a game of Hungry Hippos with the boys.

Twenty minutes later I popped upstairs to check on her. The bathroom was empty, the bath was as dry as a bone and Rebecca was sitting on her bed watching TV.

'I thought you were having a bath?' I asked.

'Oh,' she gasped. 'Oh yeah, I forgot.'

She was so absent-minded it was unbelievable.

'I'll go and run it now,' she said, jumping up.

I went back downstairs to see the twins. Fifteen minutes later they were starting to squabble and I could see they were getting tired.

'Come on, boys, let's go upstairs and read some stories,' I told them. 'Rebecca's in the bathroom at the moment but when she's out it will be your turn.'

As we trooped up the stairs, I could hear the sound of running water.

At last, I thought to myself. But as I walked past the bathroom, I glanced in and did a double take. The taps were on full pelt and the water was literally up to the brim. Another second and it would overflow and flood the place.

'Blimey!' I yelled.

I ran over and, just in the nick of time, turned the taps off.

I popped my head around the door in Rebecca's bedroom. She was on her phone, oblivious to what was going on across the landing.

'Have you checked on your bath recently?' I asked.

'Oh,' she gasped, jumping up.

'Good job I did then,' I replied. 'The water was a second away from overflowing and flooding the place! Rebecca, you can't just turn the taps on and forget about it.'

'I'm sorry, I just forgot,' she pleaded.

I was getting weary with the same excuse every time.

'You've got to start taking responsibility for your own actions,' I told her.

'My brain just gets really muddled sometimes and I don't remember,' she sighed.

The confusion on her face looked genuine. However, I didn't know what to think. Was this her way of attention-seeking or was this a 'feel sorry for me' routine? Or was it all a deliberate ploy so I wouldn't ask her to have a bath again? Was this her way of getting out of it by letting the water overflow? At this point, I just didn't know any more.

'I can't work her out,' I told Louisa on the phone that night. 'She's so disorganised and her memory is terrible.'

'Aren't all teenagers like that?' she laughed. 'I'm sure I was pretty bad.'

'She's in a different league,' I replied. 'I feel I need to constantly supervise her as I don't know what she's going to do next.'

*

The weeks passed and in the background Trish was still looking at what options were available for Rebecca and also where there was space. I knew independent living units didn't come up very often and teenagers leaving the care system frequently had to go on a waiting list for a flat. That was the reality of the system all over the country.

One morning, my supervising social worker Becky came round to see how I was getting on. We talked about the twins and how they were doing at school. Their mother Liz was still very up and down, and was still in hospital, but Martin seemed to be coping and was having regular contact sessions with the boys, which I knew they both loved.

'And how's Rebecca doing?' Becky asked.

'To be honest, I can't work her out,' I sighed. 'She can be very sweet. She's kind to the boys and at times you can have a nice chat with her. Other times she can just fly off the handle over very minor things and she's so scatterbrained. It's frustrating and, frankly, it's exhausting. She can't seem to remember anything.'

'I think all sixteen-year-olds are the same,' she laughed. 'Hormones all over the place.'

I smiled weakly, but at the back of my mind, I couldn't help but think that Rebecca was totally different from any other teenager I'd had living with me before.

One weekend I needed to take the boys shopping.

'I'm going into town to get the twins some new trainers and I wondered if you fancied coming?' I asked Rebecca.

'Town?' she gasped, her eyes lighting up. 'Yeah, I'll come.'

Ten minutes later, the boys and I were ready to go but there was no sign of Rebecca.

'Come on, lovey,' I shouted up the stairs. 'We're leaving now.'

Five minutes later she came down the stairs and my eyes almost popped out of my head. She'd got changed out of the tracksuit bottoms and T-shirt that she'd had on earlier and was wearing a tiny, flimsy, glittery mini dress. It was so short I could practically see her underwear. Not only that, she had on a pair of silver high heels.

'I like your sparkly shoes,' said Ethan as she teetered down the stairs.

I was gobsmacked.

'Rebecca, love, we're going into town to do some shopping, not to a nightclub,' I told her. 'You're going to be freezing dressed like that.'

'I'll be fine,' she told me. 'I always go into town like this.'

It was a chilly Saturday in March and this morning there had been frost on the ground.

'You're definitely not going to be very comfortable in those shoes traipsing round the shops.'

Eventually I managed to persuade her to change into some trainers but she point-blank refused to take the dress off. Keen to avoid a tantrum, the best I could do was to get her to put a coat over it. Her dress was shorter than her blue parka and she got a few funny looks as we walked around town.

Once we'd got the boys sorted, Rebecca asked if she could have a look at some shops. Every child who came to live with me got a weekly clothing allowance from Social Services. I wanted her to feel like she had a little bit of independence so before we'd left, I'd given her her £10 allowance so that if she saw something while we were out, she could buy it herself.

We traipsed around New Look and H&M, the twins patiently waiting with me while Rebecca browsed the rails of clothes. Finally we were wandering around Primark when she saw a cropped top that she liked for £9.

'You've got your money, so you go and pay for it and the boys and I will wait for you over there,' I told her.

We were standing by the exit when a few minutes later, I heard a commotion coming from the tills. My heart sank when I recognised the voice. I dashed over to see Rebecca leaning over the counter trying to grab the top.

'Give it back, that's mine!' she yelled.

'You can't just take it,' shouted the shop assistant. 'You need to pay for it first.'

I could see a couple of security guards heading across the shop towards her, and knew I needed to intervene before things got out of hand.

'Rebecca, what on earth's going on?' I asked, stepping forward. 'If you want the top, you need to give the lady your money.'

'I haven't got it,' she wailed. 'I lost it.'

'I gave it to you earlier and you put it in your coat pocket,' I told her, perplexed.

'Well, it's not there now,' she sighed.

There was a whole queue of people behind us who were tutting and starting to get annoyed. I quickly apologised to the shop assistant and ushered a furious Rebecca away from the tills.

'Check your pockets again,' I insisted.

'Maggie, it's not there.'

I checked too but there was no sign of the £10 note.

'It's not my fault,' wailed Rebecca.

It never is, I thought to myself.

'OK, Rebecca, well if you haven't got the money to buy the top then you'll have to put it back, I'm afraid,' I told her.

I had to take the hard line here. I knew that if I gave her another £10 or bought her the top, she would continue not taking responsibility for her possessions. She needed to learn to look after things.

'But I want it,' she huffed, glaring at me. 'I'm not putting it back.'

'Yes, you are,' I told her firmly. 'We're going home now.'

It was enough to trigger the mother of all meltdowns.

'It's my top and I'm not going without it,' she yelled.

'Rebecca, I've told you what's happening,' I told her calmly. 'The boys and I will be over there so when you've finished having your tantrum, we can go.'

'I'm not having a tantrum!' she yelled, kicking a mannequin on display. The twins looked on, their eyes wide, unsure what to make of it all.

Rebecca was sixteen years old, not six, and despite everything she had been through, she needed to learn that she couldn't behave like this. I had to be firm with her; if I gave in, it would keep on happening and it would wear me down, just as it had her previous carers.

The twins and I watched and waited while Rebecca muttered to herself under her breath and stamped her feet. Five minutes later she eventually walked over to us.

'Now that you've calmed down, I can help you look for your money,' I told her. 'It's worth us all having a quick walk around the shop to see if it's dropped out on the floor.'

'OK,' she mumbled. 'Thanks.'

We walked and walked, our eyes glued to the floor, but there was no sign of the missing £10 note. We were walking out of the shop when the twins stopped at one of those charity boxes, the kind that has a big plastic dome where you put coins in and they roll down a spiral into the bottom.

'Can we have some pennies for this, Maggie?' Albie asked.

When Rebecca saw it, she gasped.

'Oh, that's what I did with my money,' she exclaimed. 'I put it in there.'

'What on earth did you do that for?' I asked her, puzzled. 'It's just for coins.'

'I wondered what would happen if I put it in the slot,' she continued. 'And it got stuck and then slid down to the bottom.'

Sure enough, when we peered in I could see a screwed-up note at the bottom of the dome.

'Can I get it back?' she asked. 'I'll go and tell the lady.'

'No, lovey, it's gone,' I told her. 'These things are only emptied by the charities every once in a while.'

'But that's my money and I want it back,' she huffed.

'At least it's gone to a good cause,' I told her.

If she was going to do impulsive, silly things then she was going to have to learn to live with the consequences.

Two minutes later, she was walking happily out of the shop with me and the boys as if the whole thing had never happened.

There was no doubt about it – living with Rebecca was exhausting.

As well as being forgetful, she also found it hard to concentrate on one thing for long. We were watching TV one night and every two minutes she kept pressing the remote and changing the channel.

'Please stop that,' I told her. 'You're making me dizzy. Pick one thing you want to watch and let's stick with it.'

She chose *EastEnders* but ten minutes later she was fidgety and couldn't seem to keep still.

'I'm going to make a cup of tea,' she told me. 'Would you like one?'

'That would be lovely,' I told her. 'Do you know where everything is?'

'I think so,' she said.

'Well shout if you need me,' I told her.

A few minutes later I heard lots of banging and clattering coming from the kitchen followed by the smell of burning. I pressed pause and went to see what she was doing.

I walked in the kitchen to find Rebecca had got the frying pan out and was cooking sausages.

'You've just had your dinner and it'll be time for bed soon,' I told her.

'I just fancied some sausages,' she replied. 'I can do it, don't worry.'

I didn't want her to think I was looking over her shoulder so I went back into the living room. Eventually she came back in and proudly showed me her sausage sandwich.

'Well done, that looks great,' I told her. 'But where's the cup of tea I was promised?'

'Oh no, I forgot,' she said.

'Don't worry, lovey.' I smiled. 'I'm only teasing. I'll go and make myself one.'

As soon as I walked into the kitchen, a powerful smell hit my nostrils. I knew what it was straight away.

Gas.

I ran over to the hob. Rebecca had left the gas on and the whole place reeked. I turned it off and quickly ran over to the patio doors and opened them to let some fresh air in.

I coughed as the cold evening air hit my lungs.

I went back into the living room.

'Rebecca, sweetie, you left the gas on,' I told her. 'That's so dangerous – you could have gassed us all.'

'Did I?' she gasped. 'Honestly, Maggie, I didn't realise.'

'I think from now on you need to make sure that I'm in the kitchen if you're doing any cooking.'

'But I'm not a toddler,' she snapped.

'Lovey, it's just too much of a danger,' I told her. 'It's not just about me. I can't put the twins at risk like that.'

Rebecca buried her head in her hands.

'Why am I so stupid?' she yelled.

Then much to my horror, she sat up and started hitting herself again and again on her forehead.

'I'm stupid, stupid, stupid,' she chanted.

'Rebecca, stop that,' I urged, alarmed. 'You're really going to hurt yourself.'

'I don't care,' she yelled. 'I'm fed up of being stupid.'

'Sweetie, you're not stupid,' I told her, desperately trying to calm her down.

'Yes, I am,' she repeated. 'Things get mixed up in my head and I forget stuff. That's why nobody wants me and why everyone hates me. Nobody wants me because I'm so stupid.'

She started sobbing. It was the first time that I'd seen her cry and I went and sat down next to her and put my arm around her.

'Of course people want you,' I soothed. 'And you're not stupid at all. You can be a little bit forgetful, and sometimes you do silly things, but we can look at ways to try and get you more organised.'

'So you're not going to ask me to leave?' snivelled Rebecca, her blue eyes brimming with tears.

'Of course not.' I smiled. 'You've only just got here. I'm on your side, Rebecca. I'm here to help you and you're certainly not stupid.'

But as I gave her a hug, I wasn't sure if she truly believed me.

FOUR

Searching for Answers

I glanced anxiously at the front door as I pulled up outside my house.

'It's OK,' sighed Ethan from the back of the car. 'She's not there.'

I felt my shoulders sag with relief. I'd taken the twins to a contact session with their dad after school. Liz was still in hospital and their social worker didn't think she was strong enough to see the boys but they'd enjoyed the time with their dad. The session had overrun and I'd panicked as I knew Rebecca was due back from work at five and she didn't have a key.

'Where is she?' sighed Albie.

'The bus is probably running a bit late, sweetie,' I told him. 'I'm sure she'll be here soon.'

However, by six o'clock the pasta I'd made for dinner was almost ready and there was still no sign of her. Thankfully she had her mobile with her so I rang it but it went straight to voicemail.

Are you on your way home? I texted her. *Let me know.*

But there was no reply.

By seven, the boys and I had had our dinner and I was starting to get concerned. I had the number for the salon but when I rang it clicked straight onto an answer-machine message telling me that they were closed.

I told myself not to panic. Rebecca was sixteen, nearly seventeen, and she had done this before. I concentrated on getting the twins to bed before I made any calls. But even as I gave them a bath, I had one ear listening out for the sound of her coming in the front door.

By half past eight when the boys were in bed and there was still no sign of her, I knew it was time to ring it in. I called my agency's out-of-hours number and reported it to a duty social worker.

'I haven't seen her since this morning,' I told him. 'She's normally back from work at five o'clock.'

'I'll call Social Services and let them know,' the duty social worker told me.

We agreed that if Rebecca wasn't back by 10 p.m. then I would call him back and then report her to the police as a missing person.

I put the TV on to pass the time but I couldn't concentrate on anything. I felt sick. I knew a teenager who had only been missing a few hours wouldn't be a huge priority for the police so I didn't expect to hear from them for a while even if Social Services had called them.

Just before ten, there was a knock on the front door. I ran to it to find a chirpy-looking Rebecca standing there.

'Hi, Maggie.' She smiled, sauntering in like she didn't have a care in the world.

'Rebecca, where on earth have you been?' I asked her. 'I was expecting you back after work.'

'Oh, I got paid today so I got the bus into town to buy some make-up,' she told me. 'Then I got talking to some girls in the shop. I bought them some perfume cos they couldn't afford it and they said I could come back to their flat.'

My heart sank.

'Did you know these girls?' I asked her. 'How old were they?'

'Dunno,' she sighed. 'Eighteen or nineteen. I didn't know them but they seemed nice.'

All sorts of horrible scenarios flashed through my mind – drink, drugs, boys.

'It's important that you tell me exactly what you did at their flat,' I told her firmly. 'Were they kind to you?'

'Yeah, they were cool,' she said, her tone making it clear that she couldn't understand what all the fuss was about. 'We ate sweets and watched telly. They had some lager but I didn't have none because I didn't like the taste.'

'Were there any boys there?'

'Nah,' she said, shaking her head. 'Just us. It's OK, Maggie, they're my friends.'

It was unbelievable that she seemed to have no sense of stranger danger. She didn't know these girls. They could have been anyone and they had clearly taken advantage of her by asking her to buy them perfume.

She was so vulnerable and anything could have happened to her.

'Rebecca, lovey, you can't just go back with people that you don't know,' I told her gently. 'Not everyone is honest and nice. And you certainly shouldn't be spending your wages buying strangers perfume.'

I also told her that if her plans changed and she wasn't coming straight home after work then she needed to ask me first.

'I was worried sick,' I told her. 'I've been ringing your phone – didn't you hear it?'

'Were you?' she said, surprised.

She rummaged in her bag for it.

'Oh yeah, it's out of battery,' she said.

It was becoming abundantly clear how naïve Rebecca was. She wasn't streetwise and she didn't seem to have any concept of time, or of personal safety or danger.

'It's like she's away with the fairies,' I told Trish when she popped round the following day for a catch-up. 'She couldn't understand why I might have been worried or concerned that she hadn't come straight home after work.

'And as for buying perfume for those girls and then going back with them . . .'

'I know.' Trish shuddered. 'Anything could have happened to her.'

Rebecca was nearly seventeen; ordinarily, if I was fostering a child of that age, I would allow them a certain amount of freedom. With Rebecca, though, I just couldn't risk it. It seemed clear that she couldn't cope with it.

'I worry for her safety,' I told Trish. 'She's very impulsive and she's the sort of girl that other people take advantage of. It would be so easy for her to get herself into some dangerous situations.'

'I agree.' Trish nodded. 'It's becoming increasingly clear that at this stage independent living isn't going to be right for her.'

But the problem was, what *was* going to be right for her? We were eight weeks down the line now and Rebecca kept asking what was going to happen to her but at this stage, nobody seemed to be any closer to knowing.

'I honestly think she needs constant supervision,' I told Trish.

She'd done so many dangerous and careless things at my house, I had to watch her like a hawk.

'How are the temper tantrums?' asked Trish.

'Still happening,' I sighed. 'She's very up and down and she'll suddenly kick off about something very minor.'

But she was a real contradiction. Sometimes, when the twins were in bed, we'd sit and watch TV together and for a short period of time she would be calm and we could have a nice chat.

One night she had been in her room when she wandered into the living room where I was watching TV.

'Are you OK, lovey?' I smiled as she came and sat next to me on the sofa.

'Why's that lady on TV crying?' she asked me.

'Oh, they've just reunited her with her mum who she hadn't seen for many years,' I told her. 'And the other lady is her sister who she didn't know that she had. I can put something else on if you want?'

'No, it's OK,' she replied.

She was unusually quiet for the rest of the programme. Then as the credits were rolling, she turned to me.

'Could I do that, Maggie?' she asked.

'Do what, sweetie?' I replied.

'Find my mum.'

It was such a surprise, I wasn't sure what to say.

'Er yes, I suppose you could,' I told her. 'But I didn't think that you wanted to see her any more.'

'I don't mean my adopted mum, I mean my real mum,' she said. 'You know the one that gave me up when I was a baby. Can I find her like that woman did on the programme?'

The one thing Rebecca had never mentioned was her birth mother.

I switched off the TV and turned to face her.

'It's not something that I could do,' I told her. 'But if you're serious about it then we need to talk to Trish as it's your social worker who has to set the wheels in motion.'

'OK,' she said matter-of-factly. 'Please can you ask her to find my mum?'

Once Rebecca had been adopted as a baby, her records would have been closed and the only way to get them opened was for Trish to go back to the original local authority that organised the adoption. It's something that can be done at any time as long as social workers believe there's a good enough reason.

'One thing Trish is going to ask you is why do you want to find your mum?' I asked her. 'Why now?'

She shrugged.

'I didn't know I could do it,' she said. 'I just want to find her. I wanna know what she's like and where I've come from.'

In a way I was glad that she was being open and honest about it. Sometimes children took it upon themselves to find their birth parents on social media without their foster carers knowing, which could end really badly.

Another part of me knew how fickle and flighty Rebecca was. I wasn't sure whether this was just a spur of the moment thing she had decided while she was watching the programme or whether it was something that she genuinely wanted to do.

I decided to give it a few days before I said anything to Trish to see if Rebecca mentioned it again. I was convinced it was something she would quickly forget about.

However, the following day she came home from work, put her bag down and asked, 'Did you talk to Trish about finding my mum? What did she say?'

'Not yet,' I replied. 'But I will do.'

When she asked again the following day, I realised that this was something she wasn't going to forget.

I called Trish the following day.

'What?' she said, sounding surprised. 'Why now? It's not something she's ever asked about before.'

'Well, I suppose you're deciding what's going to happen to her in the future and perhaps it's got her thinking about her past and she just wants to know where she's come from,' I replied. 'I think perhaps it might help her.'

Everything else in her life was being decided for her so perhaps this was Rebecca's way of gaining some control back.

'I'll have a look in her files and see if I can find out which authority organised her original adoption,' she told me. 'I'll also need to have a chat to Rebecca just to prepare her. I'm worried that she won't be able to cope with more rejection.'

I'd supported several foster children who had wanted to look for their biological parents over the years and in my experience, it very rarely ended up in a joyful reunion like the one Rebecca had watched on the TV programme. Difficult though it might be, she needed to know the realities of what could happen.

Trish agreed to come round the following day. The salon where Rebecca worked closed at midday on Wednesdays so she would be here in the afternoon and the boys would be at school, which meant that the house would be quiet.

When she came home and saw Trish, her face lit up.

'Did Maggie ask you?' she asked. 'Did she tell you I wanted to find my real mum?'

'Yes, Maggie told me that it was something you were interested in doing,' replied Trish. 'We're happy to help you do it, but I'm afraid it's not going to be something that happens overnight.'

She explained that it might take a few weeks for her to contact the local authority and for them to find her original records before Trish could try and trace her birth mother.

'There are a few things that are really important for you to know before I do this,' she explained. 'One is that we might not actually be able to trace your mum. It's been sixteen years, and some people move around a lot and are tricky to find. The other thing you need to be aware of is that even if we do manage to trace your birth mum, there's a chance that she might not want to see you. I know it's hard to hear, but I don't want you to get your hopes up and be disappointed.'

'I don't care,' said Rebecca firmly. 'I just wanna know.'

The wheels had been set in motion now, but I was still curious to see if this desire to find her mum was just a passing phase that she would soon forget about or something Rebecca would persevere with. But to my surprise, as the days passed, the first question Rebecca would ask each evening when she got home from work was if there had been any news. She'd become fixated on it and all I could hope was that her question would soon be answered.

One day, a couple of weeks later, I was doing a spring clean when there was a knock on the door. It was Trish. It wasn't like her to come round unannounced. She was normally very bubbly and smiley but I could tell by the look on her face that there was something amiss.

'What is it?' I asked, my heart sinking. 'What's happened?'

'Can I come in, Maggie? I'll explain,' she told me.

I made us a coffee and we sat down together in the kitchen.

'Have you found Rebecca's mum?' I asked, my shoulders tensed. 'Does she not want to see her?'

Trish nodded.

'I've found her,' she said. 'Once I had her details it was relatively easy to trace her through the benefits office.

'It's not that she doesn't want to be found, Maggie.'

She paused.

'Unfortunately she's dead.'

My heart sank as Trish continued.

'Her benefits stopped three years ago. She was only thirty-two, but apparently she died of liver failure.'

'That's so sad,' I sighed.

All I could think about was how disappointed Rebecca was going to be.

'Are you going to tell Rebecca?' I asked.

'I think we have to,' she replied. 'However, it's not all bad news.

'I also managed to trace her mum's husband John, and he's said that he'd be willing to meet Rebecca and answer any questions she might have about her mum if we think it would help.'

'Is he Rebecca's biological dad?' I asked.

'No, I'm afraid not,' sighed Trish. 'He met Zoe quite a few years after she'd had Rebecca. There's no father named on her birth certificate and John says she was in quite a few casual relationships at the time.'

My head whirred with everything Trish was saying. Hearing all this was a lot for me to take on board, never mind Rebecca, and I wasn't sure how she was going to handle the news.

The twins were having a contact session with their dad after school so Trish was there when Rebecca came home from work.

'Lovey, Trish has some news for you,' I told Rebecca once she'd sat down with us in the kitchen.

Her face lit up.

'Have you found my mum? What did she say? Where does she live?' she babbled excitedly.

Trish and I gave each other a worried look that Rebecca immediately noticed.

'Oh,' she sighed. 'She doesn't want to see me, does she?'

'It's not that,' Trish explained gently. 'I'm afraid I've got some really sad news for you, Rebecca. Your biological mum Zoe died three years ago. She had liver failure.'

Rebecca looked blank.

'Oh,' she said, sounding offhand. 'That is sad.'

'Your mum got married a few years ago, and her husband John has kindly offered to meet you if you'd like to talk to him about your mum.'

'Is he my dad?' Rebecca asked, her eyes lighting up.

'No, Rebecca. He met your mum several years after you were born,' Trish told her. 'We don't know who your dad is, I'm afraid, as there wasn't a name on your birth certificate.'

'Then why would I wanna meet him then?' she scoffed.

'Lovey, he knew your mum so he would be able to tell you all about her and answer any questions that you might have,' I explained. 'You don't have to, of course, but it might help give you a sense of your mum and the kind of person that she was.'

'I suppose I'll do it then.' She shrugged.

I was pleased that she had taken up the offer but I was nervous, not only about what John was going to tell us but also about how Rebecca was going to react. I couldn't help but wonder what this was all going to mean for her, her state of mind and her future, and I couldn't help but worry about what secrets we might be about to discover.

FIVE

Secrets of the Past

In all of the weeks she'd been living with me, I'd never known Rebecca to be so quiet. She looked small and scared as she hesitated in the doorway of the café.

I took her hand in mine and gave it a squeeze.

'It's OK, sweetie,' I reassured her. 'I know you're nervous but Trish and I are here. We'll only stay as long as you want to.'

We were here to meet her biological mother's husband, John. Rebecca had taken the day off work and the twins were at school. We'd arranged to meet him in a neutral place so everyone could leave when they wanted to. John lived over 150 miles away, but he'd kindly agreed to meet us in a town that was just over an hour's drive from my house.

'There he is,' said Trish, pointing to a table in the corner where a man with a beard and a checked shirt sat. As we walked over, he did a double take.

'Wow,' he gasped. 'You must be Rebecca. You look just like your mum.'

'Do I?' she said eagerly.

'It's uncanny,' he gulped. 'You've got the same hair.'

Trish had already met John, but she introduced us.

'This is Maggie, Rebecca's current foster carer,' she explained.

'Thank you for agreeing to meet us.' I nodded. 'And you already know who Rebecca is.'

She gave him a nervous smile.

'John, we thought it might be helpful for Rebecca to hear a little bit about her mum and what she was like,' Trish said.

He sighed and I could see his eyes well up with tears.

'Zoe was great,' he sighed. 'She was funny and chatty and she had lots of friends. She was the sort of person people wanted to be around. She was kind too.'

He hesitated.

'What kind of stuff do you want to know?' he asked.

Rebecca had been quiet up until now.

'Did she ever talk about me?' she asked shyly.

'All the time.' He smiled. 'When we first met, she told me about you and she often mentioned you, especially on your birthday. I know she found that day really hard and she was always very sad and tearful. She always talked about trying to trace you when you turned eighteen.'

He put his hand into his pocket and pulled out a crumpled blurred photo of a tiny baby wrapped in a blanket.

'Is that me?' gasped Rebecca, and John nodded.

'That's the only photo she had of you. One of the nurses took it for her in the hospital when you were born. She always carried that picture round in her purse, which is why it's all scrunched up.'

'I've never seen a photo of me as a tiny baby before,' Rebecca exclaimed, looking awed.

'You can have it if you want,' John told her.

It was clear that Rebecca was thrilled.

'Why couldn't she look after me?' she asked suddenly. 'Why did she give me away?'

'I know she didn't want to, but she thought it was best for you,' he told her. 'She was nineteen and on her own. She wasn't in touch with her family and she didn't have a permanent place to live and she couldn't hold down a job.'

She looked down, fiddling with the photo in her lap.

'Why did she die?' she asked in a small voice.

I could see John was close to tears.

'Your mum had one big problem in her life and that was alcohol,' he sighed. 'She was a big drinker.

'There were times when she managed to get off it for a little while. When I first met her, she was in a good place and she wasn't drinking but it didn't last for long. No matter what she tried, she couldn't stay away from it and the hold it had over her. In the end her body couldn't take any more and it gave up,' he said, his voice wobbling with emotion.

I could see John was getting upset and I was worried it was too much for Rebecca to cope with. Trish and I exchanged a glance and it was clear that she was thinking the same thing.

'Well, I think I'll get another coffee from the counter,' said Trish. 'Would anyone else like something?'

John shook his head.

'No thanks,' I told her.

Rebecca got up to go to the toilet.

'John, I hope you don't mind but there's something I'd like to ask you,' I told him. 'I didn't want to say anything in front of Rebecca, but do you know if Zoe drank throughout her pregnancy?'

He shrugged. 'I think so,' he said. 'I know she told me that she cut down but for her that still meant three or four cans of strong lager most days.'

'But there was nothing in Rebecca's adoption notes about alcohol,' Trish said, sounding surprised.

'I think she hid it from everyone,' John explained sadly. 'Her body was so used to it that that wasn't enough to get her drunk. From what she's told me, she didn't turn up to many of her midwife appointments and I don't think she ever said anything to the doctors. She was ashamed that she was so dependent on the drink.'

As he was talking, my mind was whirring. So many things were suddenly making sense now. I looked over at Trish and I could see she was feeling the same.

But when I saw Rebecca coming back from the toilet, I quickly changed the subject. She looked exhausted and I knew it was time to wrap things up.

'Is there anything else that you'd like to ask John before we go, lovey?' I asked her gently.

She shook her head.

'I've got another photo that you might want to have,' John told her kindly.

He handed her a picture of a smiling woman in a red dress with flowers in her hair. Her eyes were blue like Rebecca's and they had the same long dark hair.

'Is that my mum?' gasped Rebecca.

'Gosh, you really do look just like her,' I said.

'That was on our wedding day seven years ago.' John smiled. 'She wasn't drinking then and she was so happy.'

He said sadly, 'I miss her every day.'

I felt really sorry for him.

'I know this must have been really hard for you, so thank you for agreeing to meet us, John,' I told him.

'That's OK,' he said. 'I'm just so sorry that Zoe never got to meet you, Rebecca. I know she loved you and she would have given anything to have done what I'm doing today.'

Rebecca didn't say anything, but she wouldn't meet his eye and I could see that she was close to tears.

We drove back in silence. Rebecca sat next to me in the front seat, staring at the photos that John had given her. I knew it had been overwhelming for her and there was a lot to take in so I didn't want to bombard her with questions. Trish had also come back to my house and she was waiting outside when we pulled up.

'What are you doing here?' Rebecca asked her.

'I thought you might want to talk about this morning and I wanted to see how you were,' replied Trish.

'I don't want to talk to anyone,' she huffed. 'I'm fed up of talking. I'm going to my room.'

She stomped off upstairs.

'It's been a hell of a lot for her to take in.' I shrugged.

'I know it was hard but I think in the long run, it will help Rebecca,' said Trish.

If I felt this drained then goodness only knew how Rebecca must be feeling.

Trish and I sat down together in the kitchen.

'It was a shock when John talked about Zoe and her alcoholism,' I told her.

'Yes, there was nothing in any of the files that suggested that there was that level of drinking,' said Trish.

She paused.

'What are you thinking, Maggie?' she asked.

Ever since we'd met with John, it had seemed clear to me that there was one thing staring us in the face – the answer to why Rebecca was like she was and the cause of most of her problems.

'I read some American studies recently about something called foetal alcohol spectrum disorders,' I began. 'When John was talking about Zoe and how she'd drunk heavily throughout her pregnancy, suddenly it all clicked into place for me. Trish, I think that Rebecca has foetal alcohol syndrome.'

Foetal alcohol spectrum disorders (FASD) were a range of birth defects associated with drinking in pregnancy. It was when alcohol in the mother's system affected the development of the baby's brain and nervous system. The most extreme kind was foetal alcohol syndrome (FAS), which was caused by heavy or frequent drinking during pregnancy. It was something that had only just started to be recognised and talked about in the UK system.

'To be honest, it's not something I know much about,' replied Trish. 'But it's certainly something that I'm hearing my managers and colleagues talking about more and more – I think we're going to have some training on it.'

'So what do we do now?' I asked her.

The one thing that I did know from reading a few articles about it was that it wasn't a widely known condition like autism or ADHD and it was extremely difficult to diagnose. Every child was affected differently – it could manifest itself as physical symptoms, while other children had behavioural issues, learning difficulties, speech and language problems or a combination of all of them.

'I think I need to talk to my manager and get her advice about what to do next,' said Trish.

That night, when the twins and Rebecca were in bed, I sat down at my computer. There was a lot more information about FAS on American websites. The more I read, the more convinced I was that Rebecca had it. Some things didn't apply – her speech and language were OK and she didn't have most of the facial characteristics. But other symptoms could have been written about Rebecca.

Struggles at school. Doesn't recognise or learn from consequences. Poor short-term memory. Risky behaviour, no sense of danger. Finds it hard to process information like directions. Finds it difficult to stay focused and concentrate on a task.

Trish called me back the following day.

'Like me, my manager doesn't know a huge amount about it but she feels that it's worth you taking Rebecca to the GP to start the ball rolling and to find out if we can get any kind of diagnosis,' she told me. 'Hopefully they can refer her to a specialist.'

But before we could do any of that, I knew we had to tell Rebecca our suspicions.

'It's not going to be easy for her to hear or understand, but I think she needs to know,' I said.

Trish and I agreed that I would be the one to tell her.

That night when Rebecca got home from work, I'd already given the boys their tea.

'I've got a pasta bake that I thought you and I could have later when the twins are in bed,' I told her.

'OK,' she replied.

I wanted to make it as relaxed as I could so I got the boys to bed early. Nerves swirled in my stomach as we sat down together in the kitchen. At first we chit-chatted about the day as Rebecca tucked into her pasta bake but I found I had no appetite.

I knew it was now or never. I took a deep breath and tried to explain things as simply as possible.

'You know when we met John the other day,' I began. 'And he was telling us about your mum and how she drank a lot and was dependent on alcohol?'

Rebecca nodded sadly.

'Well, doctors have discovered recently that when women drink while they're pregnant, the alcohol can affect the baby's development in the womb and sometimes it can cause brain damage.'

Rebecca looked confused.

'Did my mum drink when she was pregnant with me?' she asked.

'From what John told us, we think so.' I nodded.

'But has it damaged my brain?' she asked.

I owed it to her to be honest.

'Trish and I think it's likely that it might have done,' I told her.

She clattered down her fork and pushed her plate away angrily.

'Why would she do that to me?' she yelled. 'Why would she give me brain damage?'

'It's complicated, lovey, and it's really hard for any of us to understand,' I said gently. 'Alcoholism is an illness.'

'But John said she loved me,' she shouted. 'If my mum really did love me then she wouldn't hurt me. He's a liar.'

With that, she stood up and threw her glass of water onto the floor. It smashed into smithereens, shards of glass flying across the kitchen. I heard her stomp up the stairs, followed by the slam of her bedroom door.

I sighed, feeling suddenly exhausted. It had been necessary for me to tell Rebecca, but it was going to be hard for her to take in. I swept up the smashed glass then I went upstairs to check on her. I knocked on her bedroom door but there was no answer.

I knocked again.

'I'm coming in whether you like it or not,' I told her firmly.

When I walked in, she was lying on her bed staring at the ceiling. Her eyes were swollen and red and I could tell that she'd been crying. I went and sat down on the floor next to her.

'Is that what's wrong with me?' she asked. 'Is that why I'm like this?'

I nodded.

'Your brain works differently to everyone else's so you struggle with certain things,' I told her. 'It's why you find it hard to focus or concentrate and why you forget things easily.

'It's why you sometimes fly off the handle and get really cross about things. You know how you described to me that you get all muddled sometimes?'

'Is that because of my brain?'

I nodded.

'So that's why nobody wants me,' she sighed. 'They don't want me because I've got brain damage.'

'That's not true,' I told her. 'Nobody realised until now. You've got a disability, Rebecca. No one can see it and it's so rare that not many people have even heard about it. It's probably why your adoption broke down and why your placements with other foster carers have ended and why you've struggled to cope with school and at work.

'You need to be parented and treated differently because you have brain damage but none of us have realised that until now.'

I squeezed her hand.

'It's not your fault,' I told her. 'You're not to blame. This has been done to you.'

Tears filled her blue eyes.

'It's not fair,' sobbed Rebecca.

'You're right,' I said. 'It isn't fair. This is something that's totally beyond your control – you haven't chosen this. But what we need to do now is work out how we can help you.'

I explained that Trish and I wanted to take her to see the GP.

'They might know more about it and be able to refer us to a specialist,' I explained.

When I looked at Rebecca's confused face, I felt so sorry for her. This was so much for her to take in. I also knew it was going to be the start of a long, hard journey to get her condition recognised. We were going to have a fight on our hands.

SIX

A New Beginning

The GP looked up from his desk with a confused expression on his face.

'Foetal Alcohol Syndrome?' he questioned. 'I'm afraid it's not something that I've come across before.'

I'd explained that we'd recently found out that Rebecca's mum had been an alcoholic who we believed had drunk heavily throughout her pregnancy. I'd come armed with pages of information about FAS that I'd printed off US websites.

'It's something that's increasingly being talked about in the care system but I think a lot of professionals are still unaware of it,' I told him.

Unfortunately, it seemed clear that he was one of them.

'I'm not sure what I can do to help, but what I will do is refer Rebecca to a genetic specialist,' he told us. 'Hopefully they should know more.'

It was clear to me again that this was going to be a long road. It took another three weeks before we had our appointment with a geneticist at the local hospital, but thankfully she had heard of FAS.

'It's incredibly difficult to diagnose,' she sighed. 'Unfortunately, there isn't one test that I can do that means I can definitively say that that is what you have, Rebecca.

'It can be easier to diagnose when children are younger because they have certain distinct facial features,' she added. 'But as they get older, they can grow out of these.'

These features included a small head, a smooth ridge between the upper lip and nose, small- and wide-set eyes and a very thin upper lip. Rebecca was small for her age and did have small eyes and a small head but nothing that looked particularly unusual or distinctive.

'As Rebecca's birth mum isn't around to be able to confirm that she drank large amounts of alcohol throughout her pregnancy, it means that it's all largely guesswork,' the consultant explained. 'I'm afraid the best I can do is to put suspected Foetal Alcohol Syndrome on your notes.

'Even if we were able to give you a definite diagnosis, it's such a new thing that at this point in time there is no specialist support.'

It was disappointing and I left the hospital with a heavy heart.

'I'm sorry,' I told Rebecca as we walked across the hospital car park. 'I feel like I've let you down.'

'I don't mind,' she sighed. 'I know why I'm like this and that's all that matters.'

'You're right.' I smiled.

Trish and I had a catch-up after the hospital appointment.

'It was a complete and utter waste of time,' I told her. 'No one is going to give her an official diagnosis.'

'It was worth you pursuing it, Maggie,' she replied. 'Even with suspected FAS on her notes, it will make a difference to her care plan going forward.'

Ever since the night I'd explained to Rebecca that we suspected she had FAS, it was clear that it had already made such a difference for her to know what was wrong with her. In a way, she didn't really need a piece of paper or a formal diagnosis to say that she had FAS. It was enough for her to know that this wasn't her fault. She wasn't stupid or behaving like this on purpose. She wasn't attention-seeking, acting up or being deliberately difficult.

She still struggled daily to remember things. One day she got in from work and was furious as she'd lost a new notebook that I'd bought her.

'Remember what we know now, Rebecca,' I told her calmly. 'I know it's frustrating and annoying, but take a deep breath and think about whether this is really worth you getting so angry and upset.'

She closed her eyes and shook her head.

'You're right,' she sighed.

It didn't always stop her flying off the handle and having a tantrum but today it had made a difference.

It also made me think differently about how I reacted to her. I'd done my own research and looked at coping strategies and learnt tips on how to manage her behaviour. Because of her brain damage, I had to remember that I couldn't expect her to be reasonable or act her age. I encouraged her to use lists to try to get her to remember tasks and be more organised. I knew that I always needed to be direct and state clearly what I wanted to happen. Trish had spoken to her boss at the hairdresser's, who thankfully had been understanding and were willing to give her extra support.

Diagnosis or not, one thing it had done was help shape what was going to happen to Rebecca in the long term.

'What is clear to all of us now is that Rebecca needs a high level of supervision to help keep her safe,' Trish explained. 'She needs ongoing support.'

It meant that Trish had to rule out independent living and to access funding for her to go into something called Shared Lives. These were carers who opened up their homes to adults with learning disabilities. One day, Rebecca might be ready to go into assisted living or she could stay with the carers permanently if she wanted.

'It's just a question now of how long it will take to find a suitable carer with a space,' Trish sighed.

A month later, Trish came to see me.

'I've just spoken to a lovely couple who are willing to take Rebecca,' she said.

Their names were Marion and Michael. They were in their late forties and their own daughter Hannah was nineteen and had learning difficulties.

'Marion worked in a special needs school for years and she realised that once children with learning difficulties in the care system reach sixteen, there's very little provision for them going forward. They're either put into assisted living and struggle or else they're put into care homes and end up completely institutionalised.'

Two years ago they had started caring for a teenager with learning disabilities called Katie who was now eighteen.

'They've recently had an extension built so they can offer a third placement,' said Trish. 'They've been waiting for another girl of a similar age to come along.'

'It sounds perfect,' I told her, delighted.

We just had to tell Rebecca now. Trish came round that evening.

'I've got some good news for you.' She smiled. 'We've finally found a really nice, grown-up place for you to live.'

'Oh, have I got my own flat?' she asked excitedly.

'We don't think you're ready for that yet, lovey,' I told her.

Trish told her about Marion and Michael and how there were two other teenage girls living there.

'But I don't want to go to another foster carer's,' sighed Rebecca.

'Marion and Michael aren't foster carers,' she told her. 'They only look after adults so there are no little ones in their house. You and the other girls will all live together and share things like cooking and you can do fun things like cinema trips and bowling.

'You can go to work and do all the things you do now, but Marion and Michael will always be there to help you manage things and give you support if you need it.'

'But I want to get my own flat.' Rebecca frowned.

'And you might be ready for that one day,' Trish told her. 'But for now, we feel like this is the best solution.'

Rebecca didn't seem convinced.

'I've arranged for you to go round and have tea at their house tomorrow after work,' she told her. 'Come and meet them and see what you think.'

Rebecca shrugged.

'Have you told them I'm brain-damaged?' she asked bluntly. 'They might not want me if they know that.'

'They know all about what you've been through and they really want to help you,' Trish told her.

Rebecca looked surprised.

The following day Trish picked her up from work and took her to Marion and Michael's. Later on, Vicky babysat the twins while I went to pick her up.

As I pulled up outside the neat 1930s semi, I felt sick to my stomach.

Please don't let her have had a temper tantrum, I thought to myself.

I knocked on the door and a woman came to answer it. She had long grey hair and a kind face, and was wearing jeans and a T-shirt.

'You must be Marion.' I smiled.

'Come in, Maggie,' she said.

'How's Rebecca been?' I asked nervously.

'Absolutely fine.' She grinned. 'She's getting on like a house on fire with Hannah and Katie. The three of them are currently hatching plans to go to a disco next week for Rebecca's birthday.'

When I walked in the living room, Rebecca was huddled over her phone with the two girls and hardly looked up.

Michael was equally as friendly and even though I'd just met them, it was clear that they were a genuinely lovely couple.

They showed me the new extension where Rebecca would hopefully be staying.

'It's lovely,' I sighed. 'She's a lucky girl.'

She had her own double bedroom and an en-suite bathroom. There was also a second living room.

'We thought the girls might like their own grown-up space where they can hang out away from us oldies,' said Marion, smiling.

It was perfect. In the car, Rebecca wouldn't stop chatting.

'So you liked it there?' I asked her and she nodded eagerly.

'Hannah and Katie were telling me about the youth club they go to every week,' she told me. 'They have a disco and there's one next Friday. Could I go with them for my birthday?'

'I'll check with Trish but I don't see why not,' I told her.

'Will I be living at Marion and Michael's by then?' she asked.

'Well, with the current plans you wouldn't have moved in with them yet, but if it's something you'd like to do we can see what we can do.'

'Yeah,' Rebecca gasped. 'I'd love it if I was living there for my birthday.'

I knew Trish had deliberately planned to take things slowly so Rebecca could get used to the idea and settle in gradually, but given how smoothly the first meeting had gone, it seemed we didn't have anything to worry about.

'If she's keen, and Marion and Michael are too, then I don't see why she can't move earlier,' said Trish when I asked her. 'As long as the next few days go OK.'

When I told Rebecca, she was delighted. Each night, Rebecca went to Marion and Michael's after work and at the weekend she stayed overnight.

'How was it?' I asked her, as I drove her home.

'Brilliant,' she sighed. 'My bedroom is massive and I've got my own bathroom. And, Maggie, I think they like me,' she added. 'They said they won't get cross if I do stupid things and they won't blame me.'

'Rebecca, of course they like you.' I smiled. 'Everyone knows now what you've been through and we all want to help you.'

She'd taken the Thursday and Friday off work for her birthday and to move. The day before she was due to leave, I helped her pack her things. I'd got her a present that I wanted to give her before she left.

'I know it's not your birthday until tomorrow but you can open it now if you like,' I told her.

She ripped off the wrapping paper. I'd got copies of the two photos that John had given her – the one of her as a newborn and the picture of her mum – and put them into wooden frames.

'Oh wow.' She smiled. 'Thanks, Maggie.'

'I thought you could put them up in your new bedroom if you wanted,' I said. 'And I've put a few other pressies in your case but you'll have to wait until tomorrow to open those.'

Rebecca was gradually learning to forgive her mum for what had happened to her but it was still going to take time.

When the twins got home from school, we all went out to Frankie and Benny's for dinner.

'Rebecca's leaving us tomorrow,' I told Albie and Ethan.

'Aw, that's sad,' sighed Ethan.

'Are you going home?' asked Albie.

'I'm going to my new home,' Rebecca told him.

I smiled at her.

Rebecca couldn't wipe the grin off her face. She was so excited about her birthday and going to the disco with Hannah and Katie. I'd ordered a special birthday cake for her to take with her to Marion and Michael's.

'We're going to miss you, Rebecca,' I told her. 'But I know you're going to be just fine.

'To new beginnings,' I said, raising my glass.

We all chinked our glasses of lemonade and laughed.

I really hoped it was a new beginning for Rebecca and that she could move forward and put all those years of hurt and rejection behind her. Life wasn't going to be easy for her and there would always be challenges but at least now she had a greater understanding of herself and what had happened to her. Most of all, she knew that she wasn't to blame.

A note on Foetal Alcohol Spectrum Disorder

At the time Rebecca was with me, Foetal Alcohol Spectrum Disorder wasn't widely known about. Now it's thought to be the most common, non-genetic cause of learning disability in the UK. Research suggests that every year 7,000 babies in the UK are born with FASD. Adolescents and adults with FASD are overrepresented in the criminal justice system and more than 70 per cent of children with FASD have been in the care system. There is now a specialist clinic in the UK for assessing and treating children and adults with FASD.

For more information, help and support go to:
www.nofas-uk.org
www.fasdnetwork.org

Acknowledgements

Thank you to my children, Tess, Pete and Sam, who are such a big part of my fostering today. To my wide circle of fostering friends – you know who you are! Your support and your laughter are valued. To my friend Andrew B for your continued encouragement and care. Thanks also to Heather Bishop who spent many hours listening and enabled this story to be told, my literary agent Rowan Lawton and to Anna Valentine at Trapeze for giving me the opportunity to share these stories.

A Note from Maggie

I really hope you enjoyed reading these stories. I love sharing my experiences of fostering with you, and I also love hearing what you think about them. If you enjoyed this book, or any of my others, please think about leaving a review online. I know other readers really benefit from your thoughts, and I do too.

To be the first to hear about my new books, you can keep in touch on my Facebook page @MaggieHartleyAuthor. I find it inspiring to learn about your own experiences of fostering and adoption, and to read your comments and reviews.

Finally, thank you so much for choosing to read *Is It My Fault, Mummy?* If you enjoyed it, there are others available including *Too Scared to Cry*, *Tiny Prisoners*, *The Little Ghost Girl*, *A Family for Christmas*, *Too Young to be a Mum*, *Who Will Love Me Now*, *The Girl No One Wanted*, *Battered, Broken, Healed*, *Sold to be a Wife*, *Denied a Mummy*, *Daddy's Little Soldier* and *Please Don't Take My Sisters*. I hope you'll enjoy my next story just as much.

Maggie Hartley

TINY PRISONERS

Evie and Elliot are scrawny, filthy and wide-eyed with
fear when they turn up on foster carer Maggie Hartley's
doorstep. They're too afraid to leave the house and any
intrusion of the outside world sends them into a panic. It's
up to Maggie to unlock the truth of their heart-breaking
upbringing, and to help them learn to smile again.

THE LITTLE GHOST GIRL

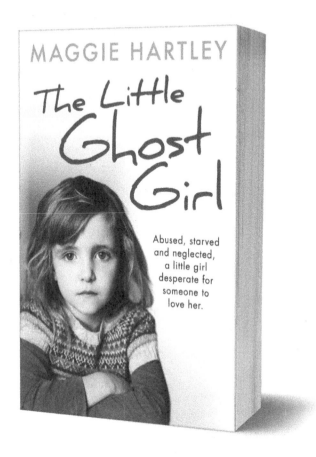

MAGGIE HARTLEY

The Little
Ghost
Girl

Abused, starved
and neglected,
a little girl
desperate for
someone to
love her.

Ruth is a ghost of a girl when she arrives into foster mother
Maggie Hartley's care. Pale, frail and withdrawn, it's clear
to Maggie that Ruth had seen and experienced things that
no 11-year-old should have to. Ruth is in desperate need of
help, but can Maggie get through to her and unearth the
harrowing secret she carries?

TOO YOUNG TO BE A MUM

When sixteen-year-old Jess arrives on foster carer Maggie Hartley's doorstep with her newborn son Jimmy, she has nowhere else to go. With social services threatening to take baby Jimmy into care, Jess knows that Maggie is her only chance of keeping her son. Can Maggie help Jess learn to become a mum?

WHO WILL LOVE ME NOW?

MAGGIE HARTLEY

Who Will Love Me Now?

Neglected, abused
and rejected.
A little girl desperate for
a home to call her own.

When ten-year-old Kirsty arrives at the home of foster carer
Maggie Hartley, she is reeling from the rejection of her
long-term foster family. She acts out, smashing up Maggie's
home. But when she threatens to hurt the baby boy Maggie
has fostered since birth, Maggie is placed in an impossible
position; one that calls in to question her decision to
become a foster carer in the first place...

BATTERED, BROKEN, HEALED

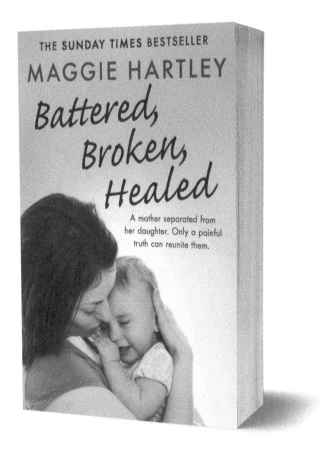

THE SUNDAY TIMES BESTSELLER

MAGGIE HARTLEY

Battered, Broken, Healed

A mother separated from her daughter. Only a painful truth can reunite them.

Six-week-old baby Jasmine comes to stay with Maggie after she is removed from her home. Neighbours have repeatedly called the police on suspicion of domestic violence, but her timid mother Hailey vehemently denies that anything is wrong. Can Maggie persuade Hailey to admit what's going on behind closed doors so that mother and baby can be reunited?

SOLD TO BE A WIFE

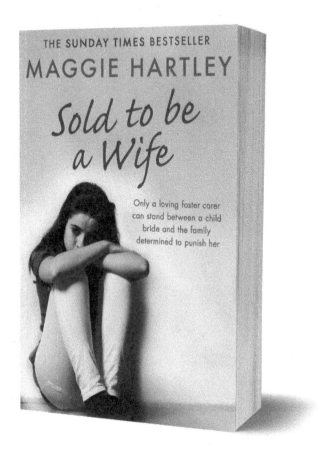

THE SUNDAY TIMES BESTSELLER

MAGGIE HARTLEY

Sold to be a Wife

Only a loving foster carer can stand between a child bride and the family determined to punish her

Fourteen-year-old Shazia has been taken into care over a fears that her family are planning to send her to Pakistan for an arranged marriage. But with Shazia denying everything and with social services unable to find any evidence, Shazia is eventually allowed to return home. But when Maggie wakes up a few weeks later in the middle of the night to a call from the terrified Shazia, it looks like her worst fears have been confirmed…

DENIED A MUMMY

THE SUNDAY TIMES BESTSELLER

MAGGIE HARTLEY

Denied a Mummy

The heartbreaking story of three little children searching for someone to love them

Maggie has her work cut out for her when her latest placement arrives on her doorstep; two little boys, aged five and seven and their eight-year-old sister. Having suffered extensive abuse and neglect, Maggie must slowly work through their trauma with love and care. But when a couple is approved to adopt the siblings, alarm bells start to ring. Maggie tries to put her own fears to one side but she can't shake the feeling of dread as she waves goodbye to them. Will these vulnerable children ever find a forever family?

TOO SCARED TO CRY

A baby too scared to cry. Two toddlers too scared to speak. This is the dramatic short story of three traumatised siblings, whose lives are transformed by the love of foster carer Maggie Hartley.